# CASE STUDIES IN
# CULTURAL ANTHROPOLOGY

GENERAL EDITORS
George and Louise Spindler
STANFORD UNIVERSITY

---

# THE TAUSUG

*Violence and Law
in a Philippine Moslem Society*

SOUTHERN

PHILIPPINES

MINDANAO

Zamboanga

BASILAN ISLAND

SULU SEA

SEA

Jolo

CELEBES

BORNEO

Scale of Miles

0 25 50 100 200

# THE TAUSUG

## *Violence and Law*
## *in a Philippine Moslem Society*

By

THOMAS M. KIEFER
*Brown University*

HOLT, RINEHART AND WINSTON, INC.

NEW YORK   CHICAGO   SAN FRANCISCO   ATLANTA

DALLAS   MONTREAL   TORONTO   LONDON   SYDNEY

Copyright © 1972 by Holt, Rinehart and Winston, Inc.
All rights reserved
Library of Congress Catalog Card Number: 77–179549
ISBN: 0–03–085618–3
Printed in the United States of America
2 3 4 5 6   059   9 8 7 6 5 4 3 2 1

# Foreword

## About the Series

These case studies in cultural anthropology are designed to bring to students, in beginning and intermediate courses in the social sciences, insights into the richness and complexity of human life as it is lived in different ways and in different places. They are written by men and women who have lived in the societies they write about and who are professionally trained as observers and interpreters of human behavior. The authors are also teachers, and in writing their books they have kept the students who will read them foremost in their minds. It is our belief that when an understanding of ways of life very different from one's own is gained, abstractions and generalizations about social structure, cultural values, subsistence techniques, and the other universal categories of human social behavior become meaningful.

## About the Author

Thomas M. Kiefer received his Ph.D. degree in anthropology from Indiana University in 1969. He also studied at Northwestern University and the University of Chicago. He has taught at the University of California at Berkeley. Interested in comparative law and the peoples of Southeast Asia, he is currently teaching at Brown University. He also teaches courses in ethnomusicology and film-making.

## About the Book

This is a study of a cultural system where violence is an everyday occurrence, where nearly every dispute escalates to violence, but where there is no word for violence itself, as the word is understood in Western culture. Instead there is a Tausug word, *maisug,* "very masculine" or "very brave." A *maisug* person is not deterred by physical danger or risk; he expresses emotions; he is combative, always ready to respond with quick anger to every real or imagined insult or injury to himself or his close kin.

Violence in all societies is paradoxical, and it is indeed so among the Tausug. They do not teach their children to fight. They teach them not to fight. Violence itself, however it is expressed, is considered morally wrong by the Tausug. To be shamed without taking revenge is, however, as great a wrong. Both the denial of violence and the sanctions for it exist together simultaneously. The Tausug recognize that man cannot be entirely consistent in either his behavior or his thinking, for there is the real world of man and the world of God. What is morally wrong in the latter may be unavoidable in the former.

The author of this case study describes the forms that violence among the Tausug takes and the conditions that trigger it. He analyzes the manner in which the defense of interests and restoration of honor may occur, when either interests or honor have been threatened or damaged. He goes further to show how disputes and the violent feuds they flare into are social processes, ramifying throughout the social system. Violence is an expression of these relationships and at the same time is contained within them and limited by them. Violence does not occur in a social vacuum, among the Tausug or in our own society. But for the Tausug the environment of violence is personal, so violence, its escalation, and its resolution are meaningful expressions of both personal feelings and of the social structure.

The resolution of violence and the settlement of disputes do not occur solely through the personalized feud among the Tausug. The idea and the practice of law are well developed. Tausug life has a strongly legalistic turn. The people are as obsessed with litigation as they are with the conflicts which make it necessary.

This case study of the Tausug also includes an analysis of their religion—a mixture of Islam, or at least a folk version of it, surviving ritual and belief from premodern times, and reworkings of orthodox Moslem ideas into new and unique patterns. The case study ends with a discussion of present relationships between the Tausug and the Philippine government. The gulf between the two is wide because of religious differences and because the Tausug, like the other Moslem groups around the Sula Sea, have been fiercely independent and intractable. The unofficial goal of the Philippine government appears to be the obliteration of Tausug culture. However understandable as a reflex to an aggressively independent and intractable minority within a national whole already faced with serious problems of factionalism, this is deeply regrettable. The Tausug, like many other minorities, is threatened with ethnocide. Whatever the eventual outcome of the struggle between the national government and the Tausug and other peoples like them, the future path of the Tausug will not be a smooth one.

GEORGE AND LOUISE SPINDLER
*General Editors*

Stanford, Calif.

# Acknowledgments

The fieldwork on which this book is based was supported primarily by the National Institute of Mental Health. Without this financial support my research among the Tausug would not have been possible. Some of the time rewriting the manuscript was also supported by the Wenner-Gren Foundation, and the Center for Southeast Asia Studies at Berkeley provided secretarial and other help.

It is difficult to single out all of the many people who helped me in the Philippines, but I wish to specifically acknowledge the assistance of Marcial Navata, Vice Mayor of Luuk municipality, and all the Oblate fathers in Sulu, especially Fr. Francis Crump and Fr. Gerhard Rixhon. There are countless Tausug who put up with my silly questions and odd habits and freely gave of their time in spite of it. While the names used in the book are fictitious, the individuals behind them are very real personalities in my mind. My field assistants, Ahmad Sumandal and Hadjan Abduhasad, helped me more than they will ever know and put up with me in my worst moments.

Many parts of this book are based upon my doctoral dissertation at Indiana University, and were read previously by James Vaughan, Richard Antoun, and Alan P. Merriam. A first draft was critically read by a number of lively undergraduates at Berkeley: Tim Bowles, Bob Roth, Carol Sutton, Bob Allen, Kathy Murphy, Greg Cykman, Lynda Lober, Kathy Ryan, Bruce Wagner, Ruth Hill, Rick Sevin, T. Nhu, and Stu Russell. Valerie Estes has also helped me in subtle ways to finish the manuscript.

THOMAS M. KIEFER

# Orthography

Most consonants used in the orthography here are pronounced as in English, although *ng* is a single nasal consonant as in "singi*ng*." There is also a glottal stop which occurs both initially and finally, but I have omitted it for convenience. There are three vowels: long *a*, as in " *bah*-leek" (*balik*, return); *i*, as in "*pah*-lee" (*pali*, wound); and *u*, as in *loo*-too (*lutu*, cooked). There is a separation or juncture between double consonants, as in "mah-*loom*-mee" (*malummi*, dirty). Stress is usually given to the first syllable of the root word, not counting prefixes such as *pag-*, *mag-*, *ma-*, *kia-*, *ka-*, and others, as in "mahg-*bah*-leek" (*magbalik*, will return).

# Contents

# Introduction

The picture of life, there as here, is drawn with the same elaboration of detail, colored by the same tints. Only in the cruel serenity of the sky, under the merciless brilliance of the sun, the dazzled eye misses the delicate detail, sees only the strong outlines while the colors, in the steady light, seem crude and without shadow. Nevertheless it is the same picture . . . And there is a bond between us and that humanity so far away. I am speaking here of men and women—not of the charming and graceful phantoms that move about in our mud and smoke and are softly luminous with the radiance of our virtues . . . I am content to sympathize with common mortals, no matter where they live, in houses or in tents, in the streets under a fog, or in the forests behind the dark line of dismal mangroves that fringe the vast solitude of the sea.

Joseph Conrad (Author's note to *Almayer's Folly*)

UNDER JOSEPH CONRAD'S WESTERN EYES the Eastern Archipelago, embracing Malaysia, Indonesia, and the Philippines, assumed an aura of mystery, intrigue, and grandeur unsurpassed in adventure fiction. When I first became interested in the area, I came across an old nineteenth-century copy of Alfred Wallace's *The Malay Archipelago*, a scientific travel book which has much of the same quality about it. Later when I arrived in the Philippines to begin anthropological field research among the Tausug of the small island of Jolo (pronounced "Holo")—an island of "forests behind the dark line of dismal mangroves that fringe the vast solitude of the sea"—, I remembered Wallace and Conrad. The main town of Jolo has an atmosphere which reminds the visitor of one of Conrad's novels: the majority of the population live in bamboo houses built over the sea and reached through a maze of shaky walkways, and the visitor may always hear gossip about outlaws in the interior or smugglers and pirates at sea. Unique costumes, sounds, and sights are encountered at every turn, and further along the coasts there are groves of palm trees, white sand beaches, and indescribably beautiful turquoise coral reefs.

1

Yet, as an anthropologist trained in the scientific description of human cultures, I knew that these "charming and graceful phantoms" were not the object of my concern. Like Conrad, I had come to sympathize with common mortals—to live, understand, and describe their culture as best I could. And while I knew that there is a tinge of romanticism in most anthropologists who travel to far-off places, I also knew that romanticism can easily turn to unproductive sentimentality. The everyday world of common sense for the Tausug does not revolve around the charming notions of the casual Western observer, but with the very real problems of everyday life: making a living, getting along with kinsmen and friends, making one's peace with God, and of primary importance for the Tausug, living in a world of physical violence.

It would be misleading to say that all Tausug are violent—some are and some are not—, but it is correct to say that their culture is heavily preoccupied with the problems of violence and its control. Law, political activity, feuding, and conflict comprise the major focus of an adult man's concern; it is in these areas that the anthropologist finds it easiest to encourage people to talk at length. In any meeting of Tausug men the conversation nearly always drifts to politics, feuding, and litigation. While there are alternative areas of interest for some persons (religion, for example, for many older persons) these alternative cultural foci seem to derive much of their meaning and significance only when compared against the dominant concern with the problems of law and violence. These topics provide the leading focus of Tausug culture. Accordingly, they will also provide the major emphasis of this book.

## The People and Their History

The Sulu Archipelago is a chain of islands extending from Mindanao in the northeast to Borneo in the southwest, between the South China Sea and the Celebes Sea (see Frontispiece map). The Tausug are the major ethnic group of the archipelago, both politically and numerically, and are centered primarily on the island of Jolo in the middle of the chain. According to the 1960 Philippine census there are about 325,000 persons who speak Tausug as their primary language, of whom about 175,000 live on Jolo island. They are the only ethnic group on the island, which is regarded as the political and cultural center of the society. Tausug are also found on most other islands of the archipelago, although they tend to prefer the larger volcanic islands which are suitable for intensive rice cultivation, leaving the smaller coral islands with their predominantly fishing orientation to non-Tausug groups.

The word *Tausug* literally means "people of the current" and refers to the treacherous ocean currents around Sulu waters. But the word also has several distinct symbolic associations. When a man says, "I am a Tausug," he may be referring to any of three things. First, he may be saying that he is a member of an ethnic group which speaks the Tausug language and has a particular form of *adat*, or custom, which sets him apart from the other Moslem ethnic groups in

Sulu. Second, he may be saying that he is a person who has some primary loyalty to the Tausug sultanate at Jolo with its legal and political institutions; this sets him apart from other Filipinos. Third, he may be saying that he is a Moslem; this sets him apart from nonbelievers, especially Christians. In most cases a person will refer to himself as a Tausug on all of these levels of meaning, but some exceptions may be noted. For example, a Tausug might refer to a Yakan (a Moslem ethnolinguistic group centered on Basilan Island) as a "Tausug" when the emphasis was clearly on the second or third levels, but a Yakan is clearly not a "Tausug" on the first level. This usage is rather confusing to an outsider at first; it took me some time to figure it out.

The Tausug speak a language closely related to the various Philippine languages spoken in the Central Philippines. They were probably migrants to the south slightly more than 1000 years ago, judging from linguistic evidence. Racially they are not too different from other Filipinos, although they tend to be taller and more heavily built, probably as a result of a diet relatively rich in protein.

Prior to the American conquest of Sulu in the early years of this century, all of the ethnic groups of Sulu (Tausug, Samals, Yakan, and the so-called nomadic "Sea Gypsies" or Badjaw) were theoretically united—with varying degrees of actual control—under the suzerainity of the Tausug Sultan of Sulu. The sultanate had its capital at Jolo; it was the northernmost of a series of petty trading and raiding states based upon Malayan and Islamic political ideas which once were found throughout the Malay Archipelago. Prior to the coming of the Spanish the sultanate at Jolo was the most centralized political system found in the Philippines.

In the sixteenth century, Islam was rapidly expanding in insular Southeast Asia, replacing Hindu-Buddhism, and various native religions in many areas. Islam was most likely brought into Sulu by at least three distinct groups: Arab traders and adventurers, Chinese Moslems from South China, and missionaries from Sumatra and Malaya. The initial period of Islamization lasted more than 100 years, and the religion was reasonably well established by the time the sultanate was founded in the middle of the fifteenth century.

When the Spanish conquered Manila in the sixteenth century, they destroyed a fledgling Islamic principality related to the sultanate at Brunei on the north coast of Borneo, and further extension of Spanish control over Luzon and the Central Philippines effectively stopped further continued Moslem penetration into those areas. But in the southern Philippines Islam was too firmly entrenched to be easily destroyed, and resistance against the Spanish crystalized among many of the Moslem groups. Islam provided an effective spirit of resistance against the Christian conquerers; for over 300 years Spain was almost continuously at war with the so-called "Moros" on their southern frontier. Tausug, Balangingi Samal, and Illanun pirates and slave raiders became the scourge of Philippine waters, ranging even as far as Malaya and southern Borneo.[1]

---

[1] Other Moslem groups within the southern Philippines include the *Maranao* around Lake Lanao in Mindanao, the *Magindanao* around the present city of Cotabato in Mindanao, the *Yakan* of Basilan Island, the *Jama Mapun* of Cagayan Sulu Island, the *Samal* of Sulu, and splinter groups in Palawan.

While the Spanish were able to establish a small garrison at Jolo town in 1878, they were never able to conquer the entire island. The Tausug regarded Spanish imperialism as attacks upon the sanctity of Islam, not without reason, for the Spanish always harbored missionary intentions. An institution of ritual suicide, called *pagsabbil* by the Tausug and *juramentado* by the Spanish, developed, and the town was walled to prevent mass suicide attacks by Tausug intent on killing and being killed.

In 1898 Spain was decisively defeated in the Spanish-American War by the American navy and Filipino revolutionaries, but it was only in May 1899 that two battalions of American infantry moved into the remote walled city of Jolo. At first the American goal was indirect rule and noninterference with the internal affairs of the sultan's government. Rampant piracy caused the abandonment of this policy with the creation in 1903 of the Moro Province, a colonial administrative unit which combined all Philippine Moslem areas. However, American efforts to capture firearms, collect taxes, brand cattle, and survey land were again interpreted as attacks on the sanctity of Islam, and several extremely bloody battles were fought in which hundreds of Tausug were killed. The last major encounter was fought under Captain John Pershing in 1913, and in 1915 the Sultan Jamul-ul-Kiram II formally abdicated all pretentions to secular power, although retaining his office as religious head of the Tausug state.

The most spectacular effect of American rule was the effective imposition of a *pax Americana* which severely limited the tendencies toward the expression of violence in Tausug society. However, as a direct result of World War II large numbers of modern firearms became available, and feuding and patterns of conflict which had remained dormant under the Americans were revived.

As a result, in the early postwar years the newly created Philippine government faced the problem of the reconquest and pacification of Jolo Island. One guerilla leader, Kamlun, was able to hold off thousands of Philippine Army regulars with less than 100 men in the early 1950s. While the central government has been able to prevail over the more highly organized armed bands in most areas today, for all practical purposes Philippine government law does not operate to any great extent in the interior.

It must be emphasized, however, that Tausug resistance to the Philippine government is quite unorganized and nonideological. Armed resistance occurs only when a man, always assisted by his kinsmen and allies, feels that he has a specific grudge or reason for fighting, usually his refusal to accept Philippine national law. Furthermore, religious motives for fighting against Christians are less important now than they once were, and the sultanate is largely out of the picture as far as antigovernment fighting is concerned. The irony of the situation, however, is that while rural Tausug have largely rejected Philippine national law, they have adapted quite well to the style and spirit of modern Philippine political life which is not too far removed from their own traditional institutions: a style of political life in which person-to-person relationships are more important than membership in political groups, a fact I will return to later.

## Doing Fieldwork among the Tausug

I went to the Philippines in the summer of 1966 and returned home two years later in the summer of 1968. My first choice for field research had been Indonesia, but the 1965 coup and subsequent political turmoil had made this impossible. I searched for an alternative field site which would meet the vague requirements of the research I wanted to do—I was interested both in traditional law as well as Islamic societies in Southeast Asia—and decided upon the southern Philippines. In the first place, Americans are usually well received in the Philippines. Second, the Mindanao-Sulu region harbors several ethnic groups that have embraced Islam which sets them off in sharp contrast to the rest of the Christian Philippines and places them closer in this respect to the Indonesian area. Third, the Sulu region in particular has long had a reputation as a center of "outlaw" activity, as well as piracy and smuggling. This fact appealed to my romantic inclinations, as well as to my theoretical interest in law.

An attempt to understand the legal conceptions of the Tausug became the major focus of two years of work. It is said among anthropologists that the longer one stays in a society, the more one realizes how much one does not know about it, but on my part I stayed until I reached a point where I could not think of a question to ask my informants that I could not already answer myself. At that point I decided it was time to leave. Not that I learned everything there was to know about Tausug culture; on the contrary, I simply had run out of significant questions!

The kinds of questions a field anthropologist asks are influenced partially by the kind of theoretical orientation he has (what he has been taught), and partially by the kind of person he is (what naturally catches his eye). The paradoxical task of ethnography—as cultural anthropology is called when the emphasis is on the description of other cultures—is to describe a way of life with as much detail as possible, taking into account the native point of view and trying to see things "from the inside out" as the people themselves do. Yet at the same time the ethnographer must be conscious of his own process of observation and present his data in a form which invites comparison with other cultures.

This is no easy task. Every human culture is unique and different from every other; it is precisely this uniqueness—its particular *style*—which is often the most interesting thing about it. One cannot let the beauty of a unique cultural style be swallowed by bloodless abstractions, yet the primary anthropological question, "What is it to be human?," must not be lost in a maze of particular descriptions. Anthropologists differ in the way they accomplish this task—the writing of ethnography is as much art as science—, and some are considerably more successful than others.

Doing fieldwork with the Tausug was a very pleasant and enjoyable experience. I never encountered any of the difficulties faced by some anthropologists who have worked in other parts of the world. While the Philippine government bureaucracy, like all bureaucracies, can sometimes be completely exasperating, I never faced anything but understanding and tolerance for my work on the part of government officials. No doubt some must have felt that I was either crazy or foolhardy to live in an area which had the highest per capita homicide rate in the country, although my Tausug friends thought I was "brave," a stereotype they seem to apply to most Americans.

Another difficulty anthropologists sometimes face is the problem of complying with native expectation of how a foreign stranger should live: some peoples insist that the anthropologist live exactly as they do, while others absolutely refuse to allow him to do so. Both extremes present problems for efficient field research. The Tausug, however, do not care one way or the other. I could go as "native" as I wanted without feeling inappropriate, yet I could always politely decline to do things on the grounds that it was not my custom as an American to do them.

Another facet of Tausug culture which made research relatively easy was their considerable patience and willingness to talk for long periods without becoming bored and figgety. Some of my interview sessions lasted a full day, with only a break for lunch. Furthermore, informants never fabricated information; in the rare instances when my questions touched upon some delicate matter—usually religion or sex—people always politely told me that such information could not be given, rather than making up a response to save my feelings.

Slightly over one year of work was done in a single community in eastern Jolo, called "Tubig Nangka" in this book. This was followed by several months of residence with the sister of the current sultan on the north coast of the island, several months residence in the town, and several months of travel in the archipelago.

My original choice of Tubig Nangka as the sample community for my study was made with the help of the local elected official who wanted to place me in an area which was relatively peaceful at the time. The irony of this choice—in many respects advantageous as far as my research was concerned—was that shortly after moving into my newly constructed house, many of the young men of Tubig Nangka became involved in a very protracted and ramified feud with a neighboring community which lasted during my entire stay. While it can be a bit unnerving to wake up to gunfire at unexpected times in the middle of the night, there were only two or three occasions when I felt genuine danger of being accidentally hit by a stray bullet. I never felt any danger of being personally attacked and scrupulously avoided taking sides in any active manner. Actually, avoidance of involvement was quite easy for the role of the *neutral* is well recognized in Tausug culture, and in most instances I had friends among the enemies of the people of Tubig Nangka, thus allowing me to travel freely.

I made use of the services of two English-speaking interpreters, both students from the town. One worked full time transcribing and translating texts: songs and poetry, folktales,· religious writings, and native court cases. The other helped me in day to day activities. After six months I knew the language well enough to operate on my own in everyday activities and conversation, although for complicated political or religious discussions I always found an interpreter helpful.

The first few weeks in Tubig Nangka were spent getting acquainted. The headman introduced me to some of the influential men in the community, and I spent several days going from house to house taking a simple census: enumerating the number of people; recording births, marriages, and deaths; and trying to obtain some idea of who was related to whom, who was living with whom, and why. People were very friendly, but curious as to my purposes for coming to live with them. I explained that different peoples in the world have different forms of custom —a fact they readily appreciated—and that I intended to write a book about their way of life. This too they understood (the Tausug write their own language in a Malay-Arabic script). Furthermore, the Tausug are generally very ethnocentric, having quite a high regard for the superiority of their culture in almost all fields except technology. It was quite reasonable that an American, whose culture they also rank very high, should come to write about them.

I kept two basic types of field notes: a day-by-day diary of community activities, unusual events, weather, and items of personal interest; and detailed descriptions of events and cultural patterns organized roughly on a topical basis. These included accounts of formal interviews on particular topics (such as religion, curing, warfare, land tenure, and so forth), accounts of casual conversations, and descriptions of events.

In all societies the culture known to the men will necessarily be somewhat different from the culture known to the women. As a male I was most fully able to participate in and understand the men's culture, omitting the world of house-keeping, child raising, and other women's activities, as well as women's percep-tions of men's activities. While I did record many casual observations of the women's culture, this book is written largely from the point of view of a male anthropologist.

Our knowledge of other people, in great contrast to our knowledge of physical things, is primarily *sympathetic*. An anthropologist must first of all under-stand different cultural patterns as the people themselves do, by taking their point of view. Because anthropologists are as human as the people they study, it is sometimes easier to do this with some cultures than with others. In choosing the Tausug I was very fortunate in this respect, for like Filipinos generally they display an enormous joy of living which I grew to admire. Furthermore, I had grown up in suburban California and my stay in Tubig Nangka was the first time in my life I had lived for any length in a situation where interpersonal warmth goes beyond the nuclear family and close friends to a larger group of persons who have known each other intimately for their whole lives.

## Plan of the Book

In the analysis of group life in different societies anthropologists always ask at least two important questions. First, what principles are used for the re-cruitment of persons into groups? Second, how do these groups function once they are formed? I have chosen to describe Tausug culture and social organization in terms of five major facets of their way of life, each in turn corresponding to a major principle of recruitment into groups: territory, kinship, friendship, loyalty to a politically legitimate officeholder, and membership in a mosque. A sixth principle of recruitment, involving the status distinction between nobility, commoners, and slaves, is much less important today and will be mentioned only in passing. These five major principles of group formation form the backbone of Tausug society and are the basis for the major chapter headings of this book.

Once we have identified the principles of recruitment into social groups, we will have to look more closely at how they actually work. At this point I only wish to stress one outstanding fact about Tausug social life which will become more apparent in the following pages: all groups must be identified in terms of their leader, not in terms of discrete social boundaries which set them off from other groups. That is, every group is really a bunch of people defined in terms of their attachment to a leader, and the membership in one group may often overlap the membership in another group of the same type. Thus, a community is implicitly defined in terms of the headman's house; a mosque, in terms of its religious leaders; a kinship group, in terms of the "ego" at its center; an alliance group for fighting, in terms of its leader; and a political group, in terms of loyalty to a legitimate officeholder. No fact of Tausug society is more basic than the principle that everything must be defined in terms of its center, not in terms of its edges.

# 1

# Subsistence and Economic Life

JOLO ISLAND IS a very rugged volcanic island about 30 miles in length. Although there are no active cones today, relatively recent volcanic activity has created a soil fertility favorable to intensive dry cultivation of rice. Originally the island was covered with a dense tropical rain forest, parts of which still survive, but human activity has converted much of the original forest into either open farmland or savanna grassland covered with the tough *imperata* (cogon) grass which has turned so much of Southeast Asia into a living green desert.

The island is surrounded by a series of coral reefs and long expanses of white coral-sand beaches. The southern coast is heavily ringed by mangrove swamps which provide a major source of the nipa palm used in making roofing material for houses. In the plains there are occasional teak forests, and in the upper reaches of the mountains—the highest is about 3000 feet above sea level—there are dense forests.

While the island is only slightly north of the equator, cool ocean breezes provide considerable relief from the sun. The northeast monsoons occur from November through April bringing heavy winds from the northeast and a moderate dry season with rain occurring once a week at most. The southwest monsoons from May through October bring an intense rainy season in which heavy rainfall occurs several times a week and often every day. Rainfall patterns are extremely erratic, however; some communities may receive an abundant supply, while other communities a short distance away may be experiencing a mild drought.

The main town of Jolo had a population of 33,000 in 1960. Traditionally it was the seat of the sultanate and a thriving port town with a mixed population of Tausug, Samals, Malays, Chinese, and a few Europeans. At present there are a considerable number of Christian Filipinos in the town as well, mostly government officials and professionals. The interior of the island, however, is entirely dominated by Tausug, with the exception of a very few Chinese merchants and Filipino army personnel in some of the small coastal towns and municipal centers.

9

## Territory and Settlement

Tausug usually build their houses near their farms. Since most farmers have multiple tracts of farm land, as well as rights to coconut trees, located in several different places, each will tend to locate his house in a site convenient to all. He will also take into account the locations of the houses of his various kinsmen. If there is a recent history of feuding in the area, he may also carefully consider the protection offered by his choice of a house site. Heaviest population density is found in the fertile inland valleys and on the outer slopes of the mountains which incline toward the sea. Location of fresh water is often a strong determinant of population distribution: small rivers, springs, and man-made wells tend to attract people.

With the exception of small towns and villages on the coast which are oriented toward a fishing economy, Tausug live in a dispersed settlement pattern. That is, houses tend to be dotted throughout the countryside, either alone or in small clusters of several houses. One reason for this pattern of dispersal, as mentioned above, is the desire on the part of each householder to have ready access to all his land holdings. Another factor is the relatively weak community solidarity if we consider it solely in terms of the physical location of households. When community solidarity is strong—which is not always the case—, it is always due to the presence of social bonds other than the mere fact that people live next to each other.

Each household is actually the center of a matrix of social relations extending outward through several levels of territorial groupings: the house, the household cluster, the hamlet, the community, the region, the island of Jolo, the world of Islam (*dar-ul-Islam*), and the world at large. However, territoriality in Tausug culture is conceived not in terms of boundaries which create totally discrete social and spatial units, but rather in terms of the space which vaguely surrounds a single point. These eight levels of territory, therefore, are not distinct social groups, but rather Tausug linguistic designations for various perspectives in terms of which a person may view his spatial world from his own individual vantage point.

Let us consider the territorial and spatial world of Najudain Hamsinane, a young household head who lived very near my own house in Tubig Nangka. Naju, as most people called him, lives with his wife and daughter, two daughters by a former marriage, and three unmarried sisters, in a single one-room house built of bamboo and thatch roofing. He is a man of about average wealth: he owns five head of cattle, two carabao (water buffalo), a rifle, and rights in several tracts of land. One small tract of rice land he holds as the native owner in Tausug customary law, although the land is actually registered in the government land office under the name of a former headman of the community. He is a sharecropper on another piece of riceland (he has "borrowed" the land, as the Tausug say) and pays a very nominal share to the owner; these rights he inherited from his father. He has also "borrowed" another small piece of land which he uses to grow cassava (a starchy root crop related to tapioca); no share is paid on this

*Tausug bamboo house.*

land because it is not customary to give compensation for cassava land. In addition, Naju is the owner of 90 mature coconut trees which provide him with a small cash income from the sale of dried copra. These trees were inherited from his father and are located in several groves in Tubig Nangka on land belonging to someone else—in Tausug law it is possible to own trees without owning the land they grow on.

Naju's house is built up off the ground on piles to keep the house cool as well as to discourage insects, and it is surrounded by a series of elevated porches which connect to a separate kitchen. Some of the other houses in Tubig Nangka are surrounded by a stockade or barbed wire for protection against ambushes at night, but at present Naju does not have any active enemies and he felt no need to construct one. His major household furnishings include sleeping mattresses, mosquito nets, woven reed mats, wooden chests for storage, various brass trays and other brass objects, a hand-cranked sewing machine, and several large containers for rice which are stored above the rafters of the house.

Naju's house is the center of his territorial world. Some houses in Tubig Nangka are isolated, but his house is located in a close household cluster consisting of two additional houses within 20 yards. Out of 59 houses in Tubig

Nangka, 35 were in close clusters of varying size. Quite often close kinsmen (parents, children, siblings, first cousins) will live in close proximity in a household cluster, although there is no fixed rule determining house location. In Naju's case he is only distantly related to the heads of the two other houses nearby, but chose to put his house in that location because of the convenience of location to his farms. A man can put up his house almost anywhere he desires, providing he makes a courtesy request of the person who has rights or claims upon the land.

Beyond the house and the household cluster, the next level of territory recognized by Naju is the *lungan*, or hamlet. It must be remembered that territory is not merely physical space, but social relations as they are organized in terms of physical space. The hamlet is actually a large dispersed cluster of houses held together by overlapping bonds of kinship, as well as location in a common territory. There was one major hamlet in Tubig Nangka, numbering 28 houses, which was the physical and political center of the larger community. The household heads were all kinsmen to each other in overlapping and multifarious ways. That is, a man might be a first cousin to another man through his father and a second cousin to the same man through his mother.

The next level of territorial organization is the community, or *kauman*,

*House interior, with infant's cradle on left.*

which is identified not only because of its core group of kinsmen, but also because of its larger size and political leadership. A community has a common history of a single headman, as well as a common name which is recognized by outsiders. The exact territory to which the name refers, however, will often fluctuate through time, especially with changes in the political power of successive headmen. While the members of a community are more closely related to each other than they are to persons of adjacent communities, the solidarity of the community is symbolized not only by kinship but also by the person of the headman and whatever official titles he may have received from the sultan, and his house is considered the social, political, and often the geographic center. The community of Tubig Nangka had at least 59 houses, although the boundaries in several directions were vague and ill-defined, with some houses on the periphery claiming loyalty to two headmen and two communities.

Boundaries may be distinct along one border and vague along another. If we begin at Naju's house in Tubig Nangka and walk directly west, we will encounter a gradual decline in hospitality and a gradual increase in tactful suspicion; this gradation will continue until the traveler is not recognized at all. On the other hand, if one begins to walk directly north from Tubig Nangka, one will soon come to a point where there is a very radical break in patterns of hospitality. Such points are usually found in areas of lower population density, and kinship ties across these boundaires are very weakly developed. In general, the further away from home one travels, the more suspicious people become of strangers.

The strength of the solidarity of a community and the degree to which its members feel distinct from neighboring communities depends on several factors: the power of the headman, the amount of intermarriage within the community, attendance at a common mosque, and the prevalence of recent feuding. The headman of Tubig Nangka had considerable influence not only in his own community, but also in several neighboring areas. The mosque in Tubig Nangka served an area much wider than the community itself, and the headman ran a weekly market and cock fighting ring which attracted people from the entire region and considerably enhanced his power and influence.

The region refers to a territorial unit larger than the community, and can refer to a grouping of several communities or to one of the five traditional regions of Jolo Island. In the past, and sometimes today as well, a region was often associated with a single powerful headman who had acquired influence throughout the region through a clever manipulation of alliances and had received one of the higher titles bestowed by the sultan. Today regional influence is usually exercised by elected officials of the Philippine government. While these officials are Tausug, they are nevertheless somewhat removed from the form—although not the style—of the traditional political system.

The next level of territory recognized by Naju is Jolo Island, or *lupaq sug* ("land of the current"). Anthropologists who have studied insular peoples have often noted that an island environment has a profound effect on people's conceptions of space and direction. The Tausug are no exception in this regard. Besides the four cardinal directions, two major directions are emphasized in everyday conversation: "toward the beach" and "away from the beach." In addition, people are classified as either "people of the interior" (*tau gimba*) or "people of the beach" (*tau higad*) depending on where they live relative to the speaker.

The world of Islam, *dar-ul-Islam*, is a conception of social territory which the modern West has largely abandoned. It is roughly comparable to the medieval idea of Christendom: the world of the faithful. Most Tausug are only vaguely aware of the actual geography of the Moslem religion. Many regard Jolo, along with Mecca, as the twin centers of the Moslem world. Except for the few persons who have made the pilgrimage, Tausug have little conception of the size of the world or the distance to Mecca, other than the notion that it is "at the end of the sky." The significance of the concept of *dar-ul-Islam* for the Tausug is not that it accurately represents the actual reality of the world of Islam, but that it clearly distinguishes between a world which is Moslem and a world which is not.

## Rice Farming

Neither irrigated wet rice nor shifting-cultivation methods of farming, the two major agricultural ecosystems of insular Southeast Asia, are important in Jolo. There is very little level bottomland in Jolo, and irrigated padi fields of the type common in the lowlands of Luzon and Indonesia are not possible because of drainage and rapid runoff. The other major method of growing rice in Southeast Asia, especially among the more isolated tribal peoples, is shifting cultivation, called *caingin* in the Philippines. The tropical forest cover is burned over during the dry season, and upland varieties of rice and other crops are planted among the rubble and ashes. An adequate crop can only be produced in this way for a few seasons at most; the land must eventually be abandoned and allowed to regain its forest cover. This method of cultivation makes no use of the plow or draught animals, and excessive cultivation caused by population pressure often makes it impossible for the forest to return completely. In these cases the land is often invaded by an extremely tough grass which makes further cultivation difficult. Some areas of Jolo Island are covered with grasslands of this type, although Tausug possess the technology—in the form of draught animals and plows—to reconvert this land if needed.

Some shifting cultivation of this kind is practiced in Jolo today in the forests, although it is considered a low prestige method of farming and is practiced only by the very poor. Most Tausug farming involves the cultivation of rice without irrigation on permanent fields. Unfortunately no studies of the nature of this kind of upland rice ecosystem have been made, but it can be said that through a fortuitous combination of favorable volcanic soils, technolgy, climate and other ecological factors, Jolo Island has been able to support a relatively dense population without recourse to irrigation methods of cultivation and the higher yields which usually accompany them. Jolo Island has over 950 square kilometers of total land area of which about one half is currently under cultivation to either rice or coconuts. The remainder is either unusable mountain land, tropical rain forests, or former agricultural land which has been invaded by *cogon* grasses.

Rice is the mainstay of the Tausug diet and is eaten at about half of all meals by a person of average wealth, usually supplemented by cassava. Considered the prestige food, it is always exclusively served at feasts and to important guests. Tausug also make considerable use of corn, which is eaten fresh, made into a gruel, or ground and mixed with rice.

Naju's agricultural year begins during the dry season (November through April) when he must prepare his fields for planting. His two major pieces of rice land must be plowed several times in alternating directions in order to break up the heavy soil. Before plowing, however, he first clears and burns the low underbush and weeds which have grown up since the last harvest, allowing the ashes to add nutrients to the soil. His plow is a simple single-bladed wooden tool which is pulled by either a cow or water buffalo. The soil is quite rocky, and the larger stones are removed and placed along the edges where they accumulate and form ridges which serve to give permanence to the fields. The edges of fields are also defined by rows of banana plants which are a major source food as well.

Naju may spend two months preparing his fields for planting; the finer the plowing the greater the yield. He usually plows several hours in the morning and several hours in the afternoon, giving his animal a rest from the hot midday sun. After the day's plowing he will take the animal to a waterhole or spring,

*Stopping for a smoke during a hard day's plowing. The draught animal is a water buffalo.*

clean it, and load several bamboo containers with fresh drinking water for the house. The time spent at the waterhole is also an opportunity to converse with other men of the community, to relax, and perhaps to enjoy a cigarette.

Naju times his planting to coincide with his neighbors' for several practical reasons. In the first place, birds might very well eat all the seed if he planted alone. In the second place, rice cultivation has many religious associations which make it subject to partial community sanction. Finally, the Moslem calendar is based upon a lunar cycle (12 months of 29 days), and the planting date must be adjusted each year to bring it into line with the actual 365 day terrestial year. This calendrical knowledge is primarily in the hands of religious leaders, called *fakil*, who decide the approximate time for planting each year in consultation with the community headman, so that the fields in a community are usually planted within several days of each other.

The planting begins in the early morning of a day a week or two before the expected beginning of the rainy season; the seed will not sprout until after the first major rain. Chickens are fenced until after the seed has sprouted to prevent losses of the seed, which has been saved from the previous year's harvest. A set of ritual paraphernalia is placed in the middle of the field, consisting of a long bamboo pole, several religiously significant plants, and other items. The specific symbolism of these items is unknown to most Tausug, but they are thought absolutely necessary for the success of the rice harvest according to the teachings of the ancestors. Sometimes sections of the spoken part of the Moslem Friday prayer are offered as well to insure the success of the crop. Techniques of rice farming among the Tausug are quite conservative as a result of a variety of religious sanctions. Because of the Moslem concept of the polluting nature of defecation, for example, most farmers are reluctant to put animal manure on their farms even though they recognize that this may have a positive effect.

In addition to the main crop of rice, fields are also seeded with several early-maturing cereals: corn, millet, sorghum, and sesame. Most fields are also intercropped with a late-maturing cassava. As a result there are three periods of harvest: first the corn and other cereals, then the rice, and finally the cassava which lasts until the following dry season. Yams, taro, and peanuts are planted in some places, and small vegetable gardens of beans, tomatoes, onions, and eggplants are usually kept by women.

About 10 days after the first rain, the seed will have sprouted, and the field is given a very light plowing. Weeding takes place at the same time to prevent the young rice plants from being crowded by fast growing weeds. A second weeding is usually necessary several weeks later as well, involving the entire family in a very exhausting task in the hot sun.

The rice crop is ready for harvesting in about four to five months after planting. There are no rituals performed during the growing season to insure a high yield, but just prior to the harvest, on the same day of the week that the rice was planted, an older woman conducts a ritual to insure that the "spirit" of the rice will not leave for some other place and lower the harvest. These rituals are privately performed for each farmer, although there are usually only a few persons in each community who have the knowledge to perform them. The woman enters the field and burns some incense at the center pole to "spread the ceremony all over the field." She then goes around the stalks of rice at the center three times, stopping periodically to examine the ripe rice and whisper a praise (*salam*) to it. She also goes to each of the four corners of the field in order to put four angels in position where they can guard the rice against marauding spirits, or *saytan*. At least this was the interpretation of the ritual by one informant; actually, the mythological justifications for rituals in Tausug culture are considerably more variable than the rituals themselves. The primary purpose of these rituals is to increase the harvest and reduce depredations caused by birds, rats, drought, and supernatural agencies.

The harvesting of rice typically takes place through cooperative labor

*Weeding a newly seeded rice field. The device in the background is a sun-shade.*

*Removing the husk from rice.*

exchanges among kith and kin. These labor exchanges are strictly reciprocal and also take place in building houses, helping in warfare, and other activities. Each man is obligated to return to his neighbor the same amount of labor as he received, while the host must always provide cigarettes, food, and betel (a mild stimulant which is chewed) for his guests. All forms of community economic cooperation are expressed in this manner of reciprocal exchanges between persons, rather than overall community responsibility.

In 1967 Naju harvested about 30 *caga* of unhulled rice from his fields, about the equivalent of seven sacks of polished rice. This was a very bad harvest compared with previous years, and his family had to supplement their diet with considerable cassava for the following year. In addition, a very small token percentage of the crop was given to the owner of the one piece of land he had borrowed, and 10 percent of the crop was given to local religious leaders as *jakat*, the traditional Moslem tithe. The priests in turn redistributed one half of Naju's *jakat* to his various neighbors and kept the remainder, sometimes distributing part of it to widows and the poor as required by Moslem law.

Land tenure and land ownership are extremely difficult topics to discuss crossculturally, primarily because the Western concept of "private property" is so rarely found in its fully developed form. Among the Tausug, rights to land in the first instance depend on the kind of land it is and the uses to which it can be put. For example, pasture land cannot be "owned" in quite the same sense as farm land because all community members have rights to pasture their animals in unused land. Nor can water holes really be privately owned.

We can best discuss land tenure by distinguishing several kinds of rights which individuals may have in land according to Tausug customary law. The most basic right is the right of *usufruct* (or "use"); this is inherited from either the father or the mother, although in practice most rights come from the father because farming is primarily a male activity and land tends to be associated with a man. Secondly, there are titular rights of ultimate ownership. Older kinship leaders and the politically and militarily influential tend to acquire titular rights, and headmen usually have rights of titular ownership in considerable tracts of land. Within these tracts numerous persons may have various rights of usufruct. Traditionally all land in theory was "owned" by the sultan, and local and regional headmen exercised various titular rights in lands under their control. Land law is the only sphere where Western legal concepts have made any significant inroads into Tausug thinking, and today the titular owner is usually the person whose name is on the title in the government land office. Finally, there are rights of tenancy: the right to security in a landlord-tenant relationship. The amount given by the sharecropper to the landlord is insignificantly small, usually less than 10 percent of the crop. The political and military loyalty of the tenant to the landlord is much more important than purely economical rewards. Land ownership is sought less for pecuniary gains as for the political influence it brings; it is both the partial cause and partial effect of power.

We must carefully distinguish between the various rights to land which a person may possess and his actual ability to put those rights into effect. Since in Tausug theory a man can inherit land from both his father and his mother, and ultimately from both sets of grandparents and four sets of great-grandparents, he may have rights in many tracts of land which are also claimed by others. In short, inheritance laws with respect to land are very vague, and accommodation and compromise is worked out by the various heirs in a somewhat *ad hoc* manner depending on the relative needs of the heirs, the wishes of the deceased, and the political and military power of those involved. Traditionally the absence of strict rules of land tenure was not a problem, for land was not scarce. However, since the end of World War II the increasing prevalence of coconut farming for cash is presenting many problems. Previously a man only needed rights of usufruct in the limited amount of rice land which he could find time to farm. Coconuts, however, do not require much initial investment in time while the trees are maturing, and a man can plant coconuts on as much land as he can find. This has put severe strains on the traditional system of land tenure; it has introduced an element of scarcity into a situation where none existed. As a result, while serious feuds over land ownership were seldom found 50 years ago, today they are much more prevalent.

## Coconut Farming

The major motivation behind the increased cultivation of coconuts is the desire to obtain enough Philippine currency to purchase necessary items of everyday use in a cash economy partially tied to the outside world: kerosene, textiles, guns and ammunition, medicine, white sugar, tools, and an occasional heavy capital investment such as fishing net or motorboat. In the eastern part of Jolo, guns and ammunition comprise the major bulk of cash purchases. Guns and ammunition are purchased illegally from the Philippine Army or other sources (ultimately they come from leftover World War II stocks or recent American weapons smuggled out of U.S. military installations) and constitute a considerable drain on rural Tausug living expenses—a World War II Garrand, for example, cost about 1000 pesos ($250) in 1968. However, as the amount of land in Jolo devoted to rice is decreased to make room for coconuts, more money must be spent to purchase imported rice. The conversion from rice to coconuts has tied some Tausug ever more firmly to an unpredictable world commodity market, and if the price of rice continues to increase and the value of copra continues to decrease, it is possible people will begin to think twice before planting coconuts on rice land.

Coconuts begin to bear fruit about eight years after planting, slightly sooner near the coast. Sometimes rice is interplanted with the younger trees, but the yield is not good, and it takes more work. Ripe coconuts are harvested, stripped, and split open, and the meat is removed and left to dry. Dried copra is then sold to Chinese middlemen in the town for sale on the world market. When copra prices are high, coconut farming is probably more advantageous than rice farming on a comparable piece of land, and it provides the cash necessary to make needed purchases.

In general, the boundaries between rice farm land tend to follow certain natural features of the landscape, such as slightly rocky sections or clumps of teak trees on small hills. Many of these small hills, if not excessively rocky, can be used for the planting of coconuts or cassava. Coconuts, on the other hand, do not have to be planted within natural boundaries in the same manner as rice. Natural boundaries for coconut land are not nearly as usable as a means of delimiting one man's land from anothers as they are for rice land. The essence of the Western conception of land measurement—which the Tausug are only beginning to understand—is the idea that the earth can be divided into a series of infinitely small tracts created by intersecting imaginary straight lines. Increasingly Tausug land conflicts revolve around the existence of these imaginary lines created by Philippine surveyors, but conflict tends to be more likely over coconut land than over rice land. The problem is further aggravated by the fact that land ownership and tree ownership in Tausug customary law are distinct legal issues: a man may claim the trees and not the land, or vice versa.

In addition to the cultivation of coconuts for cash, Manila hemp (used in rope making) is raised commercially in some inland areas where there is a steady supply of rain. The western half of the island, because of greater economic acculturation and greater proximity to the capital, is more oriented to a cash crop economy. Smuggling is an important source of wealth for a few Tausug who have the capital to invest in the fast boats and outboard motors necessary to outrun the government navy. Cigarettes are smuggled from North Borneo ports to Jolo or Zamboanga, and the public market in Jolo features a variety of other smuggled goods as well.

## Fishing

The second major subsistence activity of rural Tausug is fishing, although people living in the deep interior of the island seldom engage in fishing and purchase fresh fish from middlemen. The community of Tubig Nangka is located less than a mile from the sea, and most men engage in some part-time fishing to supplement their own subsistence, although if the catch is good they will sometimes sell as well. A variety of fishing techniques is used. Large woven rataan fish traps are set in the shallow coral reefs and taken up several days later, usually with an abundant catch. Certain species are regularly caught with hook and line. Fish poisons prepared from local plants are often used in shallow waters to stun fish, enabling them to be easily taken from the water. Small fish and mollusks are often trapped in tidal pools and easily gathered by women or children. Large nets are used by some full-time fishermen who can afford to invest the capital, and on the south coast large fish corrals are constructed to capture the schools of tuna which are abundant in the Celebes Sea. The Sulu Sea is rich in a great variety of fish, and most Tausug eat fish several times a week.

One of the most common methods of fishing in Tubig Nangka, however, is to stun the fish through the use of home-made dynamite. The yields from dynamite fishing in the short run are quite high, although only a percentage of the fish killed in this way are actually recovered. Apart from the danger of physical injury—many men in Jolo have lost an arm from dynamite—the damage to the ecology of the coral reef is considerable. In the long run such methods destroy the reef and the cover it affords small fish, thus driving away the predatory large fish. The maritime-oriented peoples in Sulu are much more aware of this fact than most interior Tausug, being more closely dependent on the sea for their livelihood.

## The Luwaan as a Client Group

The other ethnic groups in Sulu speak various dialects of the Samal language which is not intelligible to Tausug. There is considerable linguistic evidence that Samalan-speaking persons were prevalent on Jolo Island prior to the intrusion of Tausug speakers from the north over 1000 years ago. Today on the major Tausug islands of Jolo, Pata, Lungus, Siasi, and Tapul the only Samals to be found are seminomadic *Luwaan* and various Samal groups which have established clientage relations with land-dwelling Tausug. Social anthropologists define clientage as a servile relationship in which one whole group is subservient to another in varying ways, quite often in the status of a parish group: a group which has been expropriated from its land by another ethnic group and stays on as "guests" of the dominant group, being reduced to some form of economic dependence. The boat-dwelling Samal Laud or Luwaan, who live almost their entire lives on the water, are a pariah group in the sense that they do not control any territorial base necessary for their social order; rather, they are ultimately dependent on the Tausug for certain material goods as well as protection, at least in those areas where Tausug are numerically dominant.

Tausug distinguish between *Samal Islam* and *Samal Luwaan*. The former are Moslems and inhabit many of the offshore coral islands as permanent dwellers. The Tausug say (incorrectly) that the latter are not Moslem, live their lives on boats, and are physically and socially repulsive. The word *luwaan* which is applied to them literally means "that which was spat out", referring to .God's rejection of their way of life. Tausug have a number of myths which serve to justify, their lower status. The following is one variant of a widely told story:

One of the descendants of the prophet called Fatima had a small store near the beach. Her husband Ali wanted to eat fish, so he asked a Samal who was drinking coffee to bring some the next day. When he gave the fish to Fatima the next day he said, "I do not want any money for this fish, I only want to sleep with you." Fatima told him she would bring the fish home first. When she returned to him she brought some coconuts with her. She threw the coconuts at the Samal and they became cats, chasing after him and biting his penis. He died and then the rest of the Samal went back to their island home in the sea.

Later, Ali went to their home and asked them why they do not pray like other Moslems. They answered that it was because they were naked and ashamed. Ali gave them clothes, and he was happy because they were going to begin to pray. But they only prayed once, and then they traded all their clothes for cassava. He went back, and they again promised to begin praying. To show their good faith they cooked a splendid meal for him, but unthinkingly served him sliced dog meat. Fortunately Ali said a prayer before eating and all the slices of meat turned into dogs. He was very angry and left.

When Ali was a safe distance from the island it began to sink to the bottom of the ocean. All the Samal were killed except one pregnant woman. But she was not forgiven by God, and she and her children were cursed forever by Him; they were permanently vomited out. The only other animals which survived the flood were the monkeys that climbed to the tops of trees; thus these people and the monkeys come from the same race.

This story is an explanatory myth, or etiological tale, which explains certain features of Tausug-Samal social relations: why God rejected them, why they roam the sea, why they are afraid of dogs and cats, why they are repulsive, and why they are naked (or at least wear less clothing than Tausug).

Quite apart from explanatory myths, it is a hard fact that no Samal group can live near Jolo Island without establishing a protector-client relationship with some powerful Tausug headman on the land. The Samal live in their boats offshore or in semipermanent houses built over the sea and provide a steady supply of fish to the land-dwelling Tausug. In return they receive fruits, cassava, and other land grown products, as well as protection from the depredations of other Tausug groups. Tausug regard the Samals as cowards and easy marks for robbery; the only thing which insures their safety is a protector-client relationship.

Traditionally, all Samal were said to be owned by the sultan, who in turn transferred his rights to various influential headmen and aristocrats. This applied both to the boat-dwelling Samal Luwaan as well as to the Samals living on various coral islands. In the nineteenth century, Samal islands in the south were said to be "owned" by Tausug aristocrats associated with the sultan, and this was true in the sense that if the Samal group did not provide at least a token amount of loyalty and tribute to its Tausug lord, they might be subject to raids and depredations at the hands of Tausug pirates. Today this system only operates on a very much smaller scale with respect to the various groups of boat-dwelling Samal who are found in almost every coastal settlement on Jolo Island.

A short digression on the subject of "ownership" is necessary at this point. When a Tausug says that he owns something (for example when he says that he owns a group of Samal), he is mainly stressing that he will use his own personal power to protect it against transgression; one owns something if one is ultimately responsible for its protection. This element of power is more in the foreground in Tausug ideas of ownership largely because the element of power in Western property relations resides in the impersonal power of a centralized state. We are not conscious of the power dimension in property relations, not because it does not exist, but because we do not have to concern ourselves with it in our everyday affairs. Hence, when a Tausug headman says that he owns a group of Samals, he is not referring to them as slaves, but rather stressing a certain form of authority over them.

While the Tausug are clearly the dominant group, the relationship is not entirely one-sided. Tausug go to considerable lengths to keep on good terms with

Samals, befriending them in various ways and making small gifts. Before I arrived in Tubig Nangka, there were a group of Samal living off the coast there, but there had been some trouble with a hot-tempered Tausug and they left. During my stay the headman was trying to lure them back with promises of future protection.

## Markets and Middlemen

In Luuk municipality in eastern Jolo there were about 15 major markets in 1968, located primarily near access to land or water transportation. A partially paved road runs down the center of the island and is served by a daily bus, although the road is in extremely bad repair and transportation by water is more efficient for many communities near the coasts. The major markets usually operate every day, although activity may be more heavy on days when gambling is organized. A market with no permanent gambling usually has little chance of success.

In addition to permanent market centers, influential headmen or militarily powerful young men often organize temporary markets, often operating on scheduled days of the week. These markets attract persons from the surrounding countryside and adjacent communities. A lively trade in fish, rice, cassava, tobacco, betel, sugar, and other minor commodities occurs. However, in addition to these economic functions, markets also serve as meeting places and points for the distribution of gossip and information. When traveling beyond their home communities, Tausug are extremely cautious and conscious of the ever-present danger of being away from friends and kinsmen. Young men usually travel in groups for protection, and a man will seldom travel alone with his gun because of the possibility of being robbed and killed by thieves desiring the firearm. Markets, however, are ideally places of peace and will often attract persons from the surrounding countryside who might ordinarily be reluctant to travel for other purposes. Most families visit a market once or twice a week.

Every market has an owner, and here again ownership primarily implies the obligation to protect and derive benefits from the power such protection entails. Market owners are usually headmen with sufficient armed followers to insure the market peace, or young military leaders, often with the approval or cooperation of the community headman. Headmen settle disputes which arise in the market, and may treat any breach of the peace as a personal affront to themselves. Quarrels in markets are usually caused by disputes over gambling and business transactions, personal misunderstandings and insults between gamblers, and disputes over pawned weapons.

The market owner usually arranges to take guns and bladed weapons in pawn from unlucky gamblers. The usual arrangement is for the amount borrowed to be repaid within a specified time at 10 percent interest per week, or forfeited. Conflicts are often generated by the practice of pawning weapons, especially if there is disagreement over the interest, or if a man pawns a weapon which he does not own. While the taking of interest is condemned by the Koran, it is tolerated in connection with gambling because gambling itself is also forbidden by Moslem law. Strict adherence to many Islamic ideals is only practiced among older people, religious officials, and the very pious.

As a concrete expression of the concepts of fate and luck, gambling is extremely popular among Tausug of all ages. Cockfighting, the most popular, is exclusively a male activity and always attracts a heavy crowd. While gambling is practiced all throughout the year, it is especially enjoyed on Hari Raya, the day following the breaking of the fast of Ramadan. On this day almost everyone indulges, and in the town the streets are blocked off to make room for the gaming tables. In the recent past, horseracing and water buffalo fighting were also popular pastimes.

Anthropologists who specialize in the study of non-Western economic systems usually distinguish between three basic modes for the distribution of goods and services: reciprocity, redistribution, and market exchange. By "market" they are not primarily talking of the physical site of certain exchanges, but rather the principle of the allocation of prices in terms of the impersonal operation of the so-called law of supply and demand. So far as I can determine, foodstuffs were traditionally subject to such a mechanism in Tausug society, with prices of rice and other commodities fluctuating with supply and demand. Market transactions are considerably facilitated by the existence of general purpose money which serves as medium of exchange converting one item into any other. Though paper money was not introduced until the Americans, traditional Tausug economic life was heavily influenced by the use of Spanish, Dutch, and English coins. At present all movable commodities, especially those which are influenced by world market conditions, are subject to impersonal fluctuations in supply and demand, and Philippine money is the primary standard of value and medium of exchange.

Traditionally, however, land was not subject to conversion into money; it was not bought or sold, although it could be transferred through inheritance or various political means. Land was heirloom property, or *pusaka,* and there were said to be religious sanctions if it was alienated. These feelings about the sacrosant character of traditionally held land still remain, although land is increasingly being bought and sold. However, the concept of the "current market value" of land is almost completely absent, primarily because land is only valuable to those who are in a political or military position to take possession of it. This usually precludes sale to total strangers; land is sold only to friends, relatives, or political allies, and the market principle simply does not figure in the determination of the price.

Furthermore, the market principle is sometimes lessened in scope by the operation of a concept of customary or just price. For example, the traditional payment to a landlord is three *caga* (1½ sacks) of unpolished rice for each borrowed piece of land which can be plowed by one carabao. This price does not vary either with the actual harvest on the land or the current market price of rice.

Reciprocity as a mode of economic distribution of goods and services occurs when exchanges are patterned in terms of the implicit moral sanctions of gift giving rather than buying and selling. Reciprocal gift giving is extremely important in Tausug society; a great many economically significant transactions occur in this way. The moral implications of reciprocity in relation to mutual help in armed combat will be discussed later, but at this point we should briefly discuss the importance of quasicontractual reciprocity in Tausug economic life.

The best example of quasicontractual reciprocity is found in the system of mutual monetary exchanges which take place at every formal social affair. Weddings, funerals, circumcisions, graduation from Islamic school, and several other religious occasions have a socially similar format, although the character of the religious ritual will differ. The sponsor of the affair (for example, the father of the bride in the case of a wedding) will invite a large number of people to his house on the specified day and is obligated to provide a generous feast of rice, beef, and fancy fish as well as cigarettes and betel. Usually a cow or carabao will be slaughtered; very wealthy persons may kill several animals. In any region hardly a week goes by without at least one *paghinang*, or "doing," as these occasions are called. Guests are drawn from wide surrounding areas, including friends and distant kinsmen of the host. Unrelated people may find themselves together, and this situation offers opportunities for the creation of new friendships and the renewal of old ones. Younger men and women have an opportunity to see each other and perhaps talk in anticipation of marriage or premarital liaisons. The *paghinang* also symbolically affirms the universalism of Islam by allowing persons from distant communities to participate in a common religious undertaking. The major effect of the *paghinang*, however, is to reinforce social ties between host and guest through acts of reciprocity involving mutual attendance and mutual financial assistance.

Very few persons have enough ready cash or resources to finance a *paghinang*. Rather, the considerable expenses of the host are recouped by small contributions of money, and sometimes goods, brought by the guests. Each contribution is brought in an envelope with the guests name written on it, and the amounts are carefully recorded in a record book. The host is obligated to return the same amount, or more if possible, when the guest in his turn has a *paghinang*. The size of the gathering is a reflection not only of the wealth of the host, but also the range of his alliance network created by this mutual gift giving. An occasion held by a person of average means and limited power will draw mainly from his own community and adjacent communities. A headman's *paghinang* will draw a much larger crowd: distant allies, remote kinsmen, neighboring headmen and their followers. A *paghinang* given by the sultan or his kinsmen (and more recently, elected Philippine government politicians) will draw people from all over the island of Jolo and in some cases from adjacent islands.

Redistribution as a mode of exchange in economic life occurs when resources flow toward some central point where they are accumulated and then redistributed along different channels. The redistribution of tithes of rice by the religious leaders of a community to the poorer members of the community is an example of this principle. In addition, headmen often redistribute a considerable amount of the goods and money which their position brings them. Redistribution of this kind is usually expressed in the form of gifts which do not involve an obligation to repay, but there is, nevertheless, a diffuse form of solidarity and loyalty between headman and recipient which is expected. In the community of Tubig Nangka, the headman gave the following gifts during one three month period, for which no return in kind was expected:

1. P25.00 (25 pesos) to a man as assistance in paying a Philippine government official to release a warrant of arrest.
2. P25.00 to a man to assist in the payment of blood money in order to settle a murder case.
3. One sack of rice to a person who was conducting a feud and needed rice to feed his allies.
4. P50.00, 100 rounds of ammunition, and one cow to a distant follower in order to help the man provide funeral expenses for a kinsman who had been killed in a battle, and to assist in the costs of taking revenge.

In summary, the distribution of goods and services proceeds along three major channels: market exchange, involving the use of Philippine currency; reciprocal gift giving of money, goods, and services in a moral framework of extreme shamefulness if the gift is not repaid; and redistribution of wealth and services by persons with military and political power.

# 2

# Family and Kinship

## The Sanctions of Kinship

IN TAUSUG SOCIETY the fact of biological relationship between persons (or more correctly, the culturally based presumption of those facts) form a background against which most permanent social relationships are judged. The concepts of kinship form a rhetorical idiom in terms of which persons discuss and evaluate many kinds of social relationships that we in the modern West have largely removed from the sphere of kinship. Kinship is more important to the Tausug than it is to us, not because we do not also have to raise our children in a minimally effective atmosphere of family love and nurture, but because the sanctions of kinship in their society are used to justify and judge a much greater range of everyday behavior which goes beyond the immediate nuclear family of parents and children. To the question, "Why did you do such and such to him?," the Tausug is much more likely than we to answer, "Because he is my cousin (or sister, father, and so forth)."

A commonly heard statement among the Tausug is "You do not have to be afraid to visit his place—he is my second cousin"; or "You can trust him; he is the first cousin of my father." Tausug turn to their kinsmen for solace in times of difficulty; during sickness people always wish to return home to the care of their kith and kin. Kinship bonds form the cement in which a variety of political, economic, and military obligations are expressed. The kinship idiom gives to these relations a moral dimension which would be lacking in relations based merely on expediency; while Tausug occasionally betray their kinsmen, it is clearly thought wrong to do so.

Basic ideas about kinship are always reflected in folk concepts of biology. The Tausug theory of procreation reinforces the bilateral ("from both sides")

28

emphasis in the kinship system. The child is said to be derived biologically from the father and the mother equally. Both men and women possess *manni*, a term applied to both semen and vaginal secretions with no distinction, which originates in the liver, the primary organ of the emotions. When male *manni* and female *manni* meet inside the womb they solidify and form a child. Like Westerners the Tausug also use the metaphor of "blood" in discussing kinship, although not with nearly the same amount of emphasis.

The basis of the kinship system is the concept of the ego-centered kindred, or *usbawaris*. In anthropological jargon a kindred is roughly equivalent to that nebulous group of people we usually casually identify as one's "blood relatives": father, mother, siblings, cousins of all sorts and all other blood kinsmen related through either our father or our mother. The concept of *usbawaris* is derived from two related terms: *usba*, an Arabic-derived word meaning the kindred of the father; and *waris*, meaning the kindred of the mother. The kindred of the father and the kindred of the mother, taken together with ego's[1] own children, thus form his own *usbawaris*.

However, in everyday language the idea of *usbawaris* is used primarily in legal contexts where the emphasis is on formally defined mutual obligations between kinsmen, primarily those who are first cousins or closer. The term *campung* is used to refer to a wider group of blood kinsmen embracing both second and third cousins. Thus we may distinguish—although Tausug do not make the distinction in quite this way—between ego's *close kindred* (which includes parents, children, aunts, uncles, primary nephews and nieces, and first cousins) and an *extended kindred* (which includes all recognized consanguine, or blood, relatives no matter how distant), even though the exact series of intermediate links cannot always be traced in every instance.

It is the close kindred which is really the most effective locus of the sanctions of kinship. This is illustrated most emphatically in the eruption of feuds: a man will very seldom engage in armed combat with his first cousin, but I recorded several instances of serious feuds between second cousins (for example, father's father's brother's son's son). As the distance in relationship from ego becomes greater, the sanctions of kinship become less important and the likelihood of violence becomes progessively greater. This is vividly expressed in the saying, "I against my brother, my brother and I against my cousin, my cousin and I against the world."

The importance of the close kindred was dramatically illustrated in an incident which occurred in Tubig Nangka shortly after my arrival. Asi, a man of 35, got into an argument with Ibnu, his wife's nephew and his own distant relative, over an altercation involving the fencing of a young coconut tree. Asi and Ibnu were not on speaking terms as a result of a series of petty quarrels,

---

[1] Anthropological discussion of kinship usually presupposes an "ego," or abstract typical person.

and Ibnu began scolding him when he noticed that Asi's fence intruded on the path leading to his house. Harsh words multiplied, and when Ibnu drew his sword, Asi hit him in the head with a stone.

Ibnu died of a skull fracture several hours later in my jeep as we were taking him to the town hospital. It was dark when we arrived back in Tubig Nangka, but before bringing the corpse to the headman's house, I sent a young man to warn Asi to go into hiding—nobody really expected Ibnu to die, and we were worried that his kinsmen might attempt immediate retaliation. (Even Ibnu's kinsmen later said I was right to warn Asi; an attempt by a noninvolved party to avoid violence is never condemned.)

The headman immediately summoned a number of his armed followers who were not too closely related to either of the men. The father of Ibnu resided in a different community and was sent for; about midnight there were over 50 persons at the house discussing the killing. Ibnu's father, brother, and first cousins were vehemently talking of vengeance against Asi, while others tried to restrain them. Since both Ibnu and Asi lived in Tubig Nangka and almost all community residents were related to both in some degree of consanguinity—however slight—, there were powerful and compelling reasons to avoid a further killing which conceivably could have split the community into two feuding factions. In order to avoid more bloodshed it was necessary for Asi's brother to make an immediate offer to cover at least the cost of the funeral. It was also decided, on the suggestion of the headman, to slaughter Asi's cow for the funeral feast and pawn his water buffalo to raise additional cash. However, Asi's assets were not sufficient to cover the minimum necessary, nor were his brothers able to raise the amount. It was then decided, primarily by the headman, the major young military leader in Tubig Nangka, and several religious leaders, that the necessary funeral expenses would be raised by a general assessment of two pesos for each household within the community and an assessment for some households outside the community but still within the headman's zone of power.

The significance of the close kindred first became apparent to me in the economics of this transaction. The only people in Tubig Nangka who did not have to pay the general assessment for Ibnu's funeral were his father, mother, siblings, wife, children, nephews, and first cousins. Obviously if they were required to contribute to the blood money of their own murdered kinsman the moral effect of the transaction would have been nullified. They were *receivers* of the funeral expenses, although in actuality the money was paid only to the father. On the other hand, a second cousin of Ibnu's was required to be a *giver*. The distinction between first and second cousins, then, constitutes a primary watershed in the sanctions of kinship. Not all feuds are solved with such apparent simplicity however. The fact that Ibnu's aunt was married to Asi made settlement easier, and the conflict occurred within a single community with powerful and respected leadership.

An individual will know the names of all the members of his close kindred even if they are not living in his community. He will know most members of his extended kindred, but not all, depending on where they live, how distant the relationship is, and what kinds of social contacts he has with them. A man will usually know most of his second cousins and some of his third cousins, although in most instances he will merely refer to them as *campung* (consanguine kin) when he does not know the specific nature of the connection. Second and third cousins do not have any formal obligations to each other, although there is a feeling that they should not be treated as strangers. Quite often, however, distant kinship can be a foundation for the formation of alliances based upon friendship. A person's extended kindred may be described as a category of persons with whom he may have greater ease in activating significant social contacts should the need arise.

Tausug do not keep genealogies except in a few instances where the genealogy is necessary to justify the inheritance of a political title. In the past this applied only to the nobility and a few others. Most Tausug know the names of their great-grandparents, but few can remember further back except when the name has some significance in relation to land ownership. On the whole, living kinsmen are more important than the dead ancestors.

Since the kindred is an ego-centered group, there are as many kindreds as there are persons. Furthermore, the kindred is primarily a category of persons to whom a man can look for support and assistance in both everyday activities as well as significant crises. All members of a person's close kindred will be present at life crisis rites—weddings, funerals, and the like—given on his behalf, or for his children. They may assist in fighting, lend him money, assist in the harvesting of crops, or perform countless other activities of mutual help. However, such assistance depends not only upon mere kindred membership, but also upon the ability of the individual to activate, cement, and sustain a series of personal relationships within it. One must give support to kinsmen when needed if one can hope to reasonably expect them to help in turn; in practice, a person's relationship with some members of his kindred will necessarily be closer than with others, depending on the sense of obligation which has been mutually cultivated between the two.

Anthropologists who deal with societies in which the kindred is a major social unit usually find it convenient to distinguish between the kindred as a category in people's heads and the kindred as an acting social group. For example, Tausug assert that a man's sense of obligation to the kinsmen of his mother are the same kinds of obligations that he has to the kinsmen of his father (there are only a few minor exceptions to this derived from Islamic law); this is what we normally expect from a bilateral kinship system. They maintain that the mother's kin and the father's kin are equally important in the everyday life of the individual, and they are right, insofar as they are talking about ideal patterns of behavior. Yet in practice the effective active kindred of a person is more likely to include kinsmen of his father. Although the Tausug deny it, the reason for this discrepancy between ideals and practice is the fact that in marriages between persons from different communities the couple eventually reside permanently in the man's home community. Not all marriages are between persons in different communities, but they are sufficiently numerous to create a statistical situation where the men in any community are usually more closely related to each other than to the women. As a result, active kindred cooperation, which is always facilitated by close residence, tends to slightly favor relationships traced through males.

The significance of this fact is extremely important in the analysis of the widespread feuding and armed combat in Tausug society. The young men who cooperate with each other in the smallest alliance groups are quite often brothers or male first cousins who live close to each other in the same community. Close residence among male kinsmen means increased solidarity among the persons most likely to cooperate in feuding. Imagine the opposite situation in which male kinsmen went to live permanently in their wives' communities and were thus spread out in various locations. In such a situation, a man typically would fight next to his brother-in-law rather than his brother, a much less satisfactory arrangement.

So far we have been discussing the kindred as both a category in people's heads as well as an acting social group—in both we have focused on the individual ego as our vantage point. Now it will be necessary to remove the ego from the analysis and focus instead on the way Tausug view kinship relationships as ideals in their own right.

The relationship between parents and children, as well as between all persons of parent's and children's generation, is called *magtalianak*, literally "relationship between kinsmen of adjacent generations." This relationship, which is strongest of course between parents and children, is ideally an authority relationship based on deference and respect on the part of the younger generation and compassion and pity on the part of the elder.

The relationship between persons of the same generation (siblings, cousins) is called *magtaymanghud*, from the term for sibling. It implies close solidarity, equality, mutual helpfulness, and reciprocity, and is commonly used in legal, military, and political discussions where those virtues predominate.

Finally, Tausug identify a relationship between persons who are *magtaliapu*, members of alternate generations such as grandparents and grandchildren. It is also based on respect and compassion, but lacks the authority dimension. As in many societies, grandparents and grandchildren are indulgent toward each other, and the relationship is tempered by a good bit of playfulness.

The relative importance of different relationships is also seen in the choices people ideally make for taking revenge or staying neutral in cases where a person is related both to the victim and to the killer. If a man's second cousin kills his father-in-law, he should ideally seek revenge. But if his first cousin kills his wife's father, he should remain neutral. If a man's second cousin kills his first cousin, he should seek revenge, but if his wife's brother kills his first cousin, he should remain neutral. On the basis of a series of such choices I once attempted to construct a graded series of kinsmen for purposes of taking revenge, with the heaviest obligation at the beginning, and tapering off to kinsmen that a man has only a nebulous obligation to avenge: 1) brother, father, or son; 2) uncle, father-in-law, sibling's son; 3) grandfather; 4) first cousin, wife's brother, son's wife's father; 5) second cousin, wife's uncle, wife's grandfather; 6) third cousin.

The fact that this scale of intensity of relations with kinsmen is only an ideal which is subject to considerable modification depending on the concrete situation at hand became vividly apparent to me one afternoon when a battle was raging in a community near Tubig Nangka. While the men of Tubig Nangka were not involved in the fight, a young man named Amil had second cousins on both sides. A group of men from Tubig Nangka gathered at the edge of the forest to await news and gossip, and I observed Amil standing off by himself, obviously troubled by the events. He had three choices: he could remain neutral, as the headman of Tubig Nangka wanted him to do; he could join one second cousin; or he could join the other. He chose to join one of the second cousins and abruptly ran off to join in the affray. It is at such occasions that I wished I owned a mind-

*Father and young child. Tausug believe that fathers should be very affectionate toward their children, even more than mothers.*

reading machine; although I later asked Amil why he made the decision he did, his answers were expectably less than lucid. To the question, "Why did you join your second cousin?," the answer was a predictable, "Because he is my second cousin." But when I objected that the other man was also his second cousin, he shrugged and said, "Oh, but he is my enemy!"

The point is that while people talk as if kinship were extremely important —and indeed it is—and publicly announce decisions to engage in acts for reasons of kinship, concrete decisions are always made in the context of a situation where other factors have to be taken into account. I could only surmise what those other factors were in Amil's case because in Tausug rhetoric merely being a man's second cousin is sufficient reason to assist him if he is in trouble, and Amil felt that no further justification was necessary in that situation, although on further prodding he might have given a more detailed explanation.

## The Uses of Kinship Terms

Anthropologists always pay special attention to the terms that people use to refer to kinsmen. The ways that people classify relatives together in systems of terminology vary greatly in different cultures, and the situations in which kin terms are used are useful indicators of social conduct. English-speaking Tausug have as much trouble understanding our kinship terminology as we have understanding theirs. My interpreter was very surprised to learn that the Tausug term *amaun* does not exactly correspond to English *uncle*, although they are fairly close. *Amaun* really means "any male blood kinsman of my father's generation"; a person's father's father's sister's son is an *amaun*, although to us he is probably a second cousin once removed (we are pretty hazy about that however). The English term *cousin* cuts across several generations, while in Tausug all kin terms operate on only one generation; a cousin (*pagtunghud*) is a blood kinsman other than a sibling on ego's generation only.

✕ There are 11 major terms to refer to blood kin: mother (*ina*), father (*ama*), grandparent or grandchild (*apu*), sibling (*taymanghud*), older sibling (*magulang*), younger sibling (*manghud*), male of father's generation (*amaun*), female of father's generation (*inaun*), cousin (*pagtunghud*), child (*anak*), and kinsman of child's generation (*anakun*). Cousins can further be specified as first, second, or third depending on degree of collaterality; grandparents and grandchildren refer to each other reciprocally by the same term (*apu*). The system puts major emphasis upon differences of generation, relative age, and lineality versus collaterality.

The system of referring to affines (in-laws) is much simpler. A single term, *ugangan*, is used reciprocally between parents-in-law and children-in-law; a single term is used for all in-laws of ego's generation (*ipag*); and there are terms for husband (*bana*) and wife (*asawa*).

Kinship terms are used in at least three different levels of meaning:

denotatively, what the term means in its most restrictive sense; casually, in everyday conversation; and rhetorically, primarily in connection with legal discussions. When I was taking a census of the houses in Tubig Nangka, I was told regularly that the people living next door were siblings, or *taymanghud*. This was a source of considerable confusion in my genealogies until I realized that *taymanghud* in a casual sense can refer to a kinsman that in a more careful moment a Tausug would identify as a first cousin. Similarly, in legal discussion people are constantly reminding each other that they are brothers in a strictly metaphorical extension of the meaning of the word for rhetorical effect; *taymanghud* in this sense is any blood kinsman.

Reference terms used in talking about people must always be contrasted with terms of address which are used in face to face contact. Except for the nuclear family (father, mother, brothers, sisters, children) Tausug do not normally use kinship terms in everyday conversation to directly address a person except when they are living together in the same household. In general, personal names are used to address equals. While father, mother, and grandparent are always addressed by the kinship term, all others can be called by their names, although for uncles and aunts the kin term is respectfully preferred. Almost all address terms can be used rhetorically to emphasize the ideal style of a particular social contact, even though there is no actual kinship. The term *utu*, for example, is used in address to talk to one's son, but the term implies affectionate authority and can be used to address any younger person in that context. Similarly, *bapa* and *babu*, the address terms for uncle and aunt, can be used in a respectful manner to any older person. Wife's father and mother may be called *bapa* and *babu* by the son-in law, while they address him as *utu*. Thus, while each term denotes some specific person, it also has an emotional connotation which can be used to set a tone or style for a relationship with almost any other person with whom it is used.

## Men and Women

The separation of the sexes, especially the unmarried, is quite marked in Tausug society. At feasts and festive gatherings there is little mixing; women and young children usually sit together inside the house chatting about feminine topics, while men and older children sit outside on the porch discussing politics and feuding. This separation is the product both of indigenous patterns common to many parts of the Philippines as well as of ideas incorporated from Moslem ritual and belief. It is reflected first of all in a well-defined division of labor and sense of the propriety of men's work and women's work. Plowing, fishing, harvesting trees, and caring for animals are male activities, while care of chickens, gathering fruits, tending vegetable gardens, and preparing food are women's work. In general, the sexual division of labor depends less upon symbolic and ritual considerations than upon the physical requirements of the tasks themselves.

The key concept in social relations between men and women is shame, or *sipug*, which adheres in all situations of a sexual nature where a third party is present. It is said to be shameful to discuss the particulars of one's own sexual activities in front of a third person, although Tausug often joke about sex in public and discuss some sexual matters as long as the reference is general and not to any person present. It is shameful for any hint of sexuality between married persons to be publicly at view, for a young man and woman to be caught together, or for a girl merely to be touched by a man. Tausug are not bothered by an intense inner guilt about sex, but they are deeply concerned with the public expression of sexuality. However, aristocrats (*datu*) are said to have more libido than commoners. One old *datu* in Tubig Nangka used to boast of his sexual prowess and even abducted a young wife when he was 90—although she ran away and refused to live with him. Female aristocrats are also said to have less shame than other women and to be more overt in sexual affairs. Most women, however, are supposed to hide sexual feelings, although it is recognized that they exist. If a woman elopes, it is assumed that she is more amorous than a man, and this is thought to be shameful.

One of the prominent features of Islamic ritual which the Tausug have adopted is the distinction between things which are clean and things which are unclean—a feature it shares with Judaism. In particular, defecation and urination, menstrual blood, the flesh of certain animals such as pig and monkey, and sexual intercourse are considered polluting. This does not mean, however, that Tausug are repulsed by sexual activity. They are certainly not puritanical; sexual desire and pleasure are considered good and necessary for human happiness, although the level of expectation—especially for women—may be somewhat lower than in some other cultures. Nevertheless, they believe that there are certain supernatural dangers associated with sex which must be taken into account even though they do not attempt to understand the logic of these beliefs—God can, after all, put any restrictions He desires on men. A short ablution of water and sometimes a short prayer-like utterance in Arabic is conducted after defecation, urination and sexual intercourse to over come the pollution which God—for reasons which only He understands—has placed upon these activities; failure to conduct these ablutions will expose a man to supernatural punishment.

There is a noticeable difference in attitude toward marital and extramarital sexual behavior. Sexual stimulation of a woman beyond primary genital contact is considered shameful in the case of a wife, yet acceptable with a casual partner, because the wife is considered to be the source of a man's children and not to be playfully abused. Marital intercourse usually takes place in the middle of the night when other members of the household have fallen asleep. Intercourse takes place quickly in the dark without much visual or verbal stimulation —the primary consideration is privacy and the need to avoid public shame. Men are little concerned with the sexual satisfaction of their wives, and as far as I can tell, women do not expect a high level of satisfaction.

Although the opportunities for premarital sexual play are greater than they superficially appear, Tausug culture is very restrictive in ideals of premarital relations. There is no double standard, however, and the ideals apply equally to young men and women. This is illustrated in the variety of legal proscriptions which surround the offense of *kublit-kublit*, "touching-touching." Mere touching is always considered a prelude to sexual relations and is said to be extremely stimulating. It is a moot question whether the prohibition against touching exists because it is stimulating or whether it is stimulating because it is prohibited. During musical performances of *pagsindil* (a stylized courtship repartee sung between two male and two female singers to the accompaniment of the xylophone), a male singer may try to reach across and touch one of the women. The audience will always laugh riotously at this point at the expression of the normally forbidden.

If a young man touches a girl deliberately—or even accidentally if his lack of intention is not readily apparent—, he can be taken before any headman (Tausug say "brought before the law") and fined. In Tubig Nangka in 1968 the fines were similar to those set by the sultan for all of Jolo: 25 pesos for touching an arm during the day, 50 pesos for touching any other part of the body during the day, and 105 pesos for touching any part of the body at night. While sexual offenses of this kind sometimes lead to serious conflicts and even killings, especially when the honor of the girl is at stake, there is actually a good bit of humor and gamelike quality expressed in the inordinate elaboration of petty rules and devices for their circumvention. A boy who is brought before the *sara*, or law, for an offense of this type usually is given the choice of marrying the girl or paying the fine; if he decides to marry, the affair is technically considered to be an abduction.

A variety of touching-touching is *kap-kap*, or groping in the dark. Tausug are heavy sleepers, and the one room houses offer ample opportunity for a visiting young man to approach an unmarried girl at night. If she likes him she may consent, and nothing will happen so long as they are not discovered and she does not become pregnant (in which case marriage would be obligatory; illegitimacy is almost nonexistent). Ocasionally parents may pretend to be asleep in order to avoid a public scandal. On the other hand, if the girl screams or otherwise complains, he will be fined if he does not wish to marry her. It is considered very shameful for a girl to be touched in this way, even if sexual intercourse did not occur, although only if the act is discovered. It is difficult to be certain, but I do not believe that Tausug feel any guilt over a sexual transgression which is not discovered.

There are no prostitutes in rural Jolo, and Tausug consider the idea of a man "mixing his semen with the semen of other men" to be improper. Masturbation is considered to be a sin against God, and some people feel that excess semen is rendered into all sorts of malevolent spirits (although there is little guilt over the inevitable breaking of the rule). The seduction of an unmarried girl, however, is not contrary to religious law—although it is opposed to customary law, a distinction I will return to later—and is considered an appropriate way for a young man to express his masculinity if he can get away with it. Furthermore, there is no publicly recognized courtship between unmarried young people; ideally marriages are arranged by parents. In the absence of publicly recognized outlets for premarital sexual expression, a young man still has a number of choices open to him. He can go to a prospective girl's house and ingratiate himself with the parents. Possibly he could then ask his sister to invite the girl on a ruse to spend the night at his house, and in the evening he would attempt to make love to her. An older trusted woman might arrange to take the girl to the forest on a ruse, or to a waterhole, and he might approach her there. Most of my male informants maintained that unmarried girls would like to have sexual relations if they could be sure it was kept secret, although there is so much shame which surrounds the subject that I was unable to verify this with the women. A young man might also seek out a younger widow, who usually travel alone unlike unmarried girls. Widows, however, often want to get remarried and may complain to the headman, whereas an unmarried girl is usually reluctant to marry.

Mawa, my cook in Tubig Nangka, was involved in two cases of attempted seduction. Mawa was doubly attractive. First, she was a good-looking widow; second, she came from outside Tubig Nangka and was not surrounded by kinsmen who might be angry at her lover. Jamas gained entrance to my house during a celebration when everyone else was occupied at the mosque and began embracing her. She refused and complained to the headman who summoned Jamas and his kinsmen for a formal discussion of the case. As a widow she was able to act on her own behalf (an unmarried girl would normally be represented by her father), and she demanded compensation for the insult in the form of a fine, which is usually split between the victim and the headman. Jamas knew she did not wish to marry him, so he offered to do so; when she refused his offer, the customary law had been fulfilled and he was not obligated to pay the fine. Several months later Mawa was caught having sexual relations with another young man. Since extramarital transgressions are contrary to customary law and said to be disruptive of the tranquility of the community, the headman had the right to demand that the offense be corrected. In this case Mawa wanted to marry the young man and the headman insisted that the arrangements be made.

Some sexual offenses are religious crimes which call for immediate punishment if discovered, including bestiality, overt sodomy, and incest. These sins are said to result in *pasuh*, literally "heat", or a lack of rainfall for the community. Since rainfall patterns are extremely erratic, lack of rain in one community while abundant rain is falling in an adjacent community will often motivate people to search for a guilty offender. Classificatory incest (beyond the nuclear family) is actually quite common; there were several instances during my field work. It usually occurs between a man and his wife's unmarried sister while they are living in the same house; according to Islamic law this is incestuous. Father-daughter or mother-son incest is much rarer and formerly was punished by death by placing the pair in a rataan fishtrap and sinking it in the ocean.

Sometimes the case will be "put before the law" by a witness; if the unmarried woman is pregnant, the situation will be obvious. A common practice in serious sexual crimes is for the accusation to be made anonymously by posting an unsigned notice in the mosque. The case will be investigated by the headman; if the charges are proven the guilty parties are fined and taken to the ocean to be ritually whipped and publicly shamed as a means of expiating the sin in the eyes of God. Furthermore if incest with a man's wife's sister results in pregnancy, he will be required to divorce his wife and marry her sister, if only until the child is born.

## Getting Married

A maxim that is sometimes heard in Jolo is that a young man should get married once he has been farming for three years on his own; otherwise, it is said, he may encounter trouble in gambling, fighting, or engaging in secret affairs with girls (which are not condemned so much in themselves, but because they are likely to lead to feuds). Young men usually marry a few years after puberty, often around age 18, if the necessary bridewealth can be raised. Girls marry from age 16 to 18, or even earlier, although there is much individual variation. Uyung, one of my best informants, was a very handsome fellow of 25 who managed to succeed in several clandestine affairs. Although he wanted to marry, he had few prospects for supporting a family, and his parents were unable to raise the bridewealth. While girls admired him, their parents rejected him.

Some of the considerations which a girl's parents take into account in a young man include his wealth, the status of his parents, his reputation as a worker, whether he is a gambler, and his general demeanor and ability to get along with people. His fighting ability may also be a consideration, but an equivocal one, because an extremely brave man, especially if he is hot-tempered, is likely to drag them into more trouble than they wish. The daughter is not normally consulted; usually her parents do not care if she likes the young man or not, thinking that their decision is for the best.

Islamic marriage ritual is framed as a contract between the young man and the girl's father (second marriages are an exception); this masculine emphasis runs throughout all phases leading up to marriage as well. The girl, especially if she has never been married before, is largely out of the picture. Her desires are for the most part ignored, while the young man has much greater freedom of choice. It is almost impossible for parents to arrange a marriage completely against the will of their son, but daughters are often persuaded into undesired unions. To understand this fact in proper perspective, we must remember that in Tausug society, as in most traditional societies, men and women have a wide variety of warm and meaningful social contacts through institutions other than marriage: close friends, neighbors, alliance groups, and others. A forced undesired marriage in our society would be intolerable precisely because meaningful interpersonal relations outside of marriage have become increasingly ephemeral; marriage is all that we have got, and we expect a great deal of it. The Tausug expect less and thus are able to tolerate arrangements which might be unsatisfactory to us.

Tausug marriage customs are complicated by many recognized alternative patterns, with people manipulating the rules for their own advantage. Basically there are three major modes of marriage: regular marriage by negotiation between the respective kindreds, elopement, and abduction.

The ideal marriage is arranged by the parents of the couple. Usually the boy will privately suggest the name of a likely girl to his parents; in any event they will usually ask his opinion before proceeding further. If they dislike his choice, he can always abduct her; if they insist that he marry an undesirable girl, he can threaten to run away from home, or run amuck, or become an outlaw. About half of all arranged marriages are contracted between close kin, usually first or second cousins. A marriage with a first cousin is considered ideal for several reasons. First, there is the ease of negotiation when the transaction is arranged between the parents (who would be siblings) of first cousins. Quite often a very high bridewealth can be publicly announced, which looks good and enhances the prestige of the parties when in fact they have privately agreed to a lesser sum. Second, marriage between close kinsmen simplifies the inheritance of land. Third, it is said that parents can jointly exert a stabilizing influence on the marriage.

Once the choice of a girl has been determined, the first step is the formal request of marriage, or *pagpangasawa*. When Nain's mother Bulayla decided to ask for the hand of Adjibun's daughter, she was assisted by about 25 close kin who gathered in her house one evening. It was necessary to put the public negotiations in the hand of a male kinsmen of Nain's dead father, since it is legal fiction in Tausug marriage law that negotiations should be between the girl's father and the boy's father. Early in the evening the group left for Adjibun's house amid much yelling and merrymaking. Although Adjibun had heard rumors that they were coming, he feigned surprise when they arrived. After the entire group had crowded into the house, Ajamuddin, the negotiator for Nain, threw a gold coin on the floor and announced, "We are here to ask for the hand of Sittikarma on behalf of Nain, and this coin will indicate our sincerity." It was later decided to have a formal *isun*, or conference, the following week to hear Adjibun's demands for the bridewealth. The initial ceremony was only a stylized formality, devoid of much content, and lasted less than one hour.

The following Thursday the *isun* was held at Adjibun's house to present the demands for bridewealth. By this time he and the other close kin of the girl had time to discuss the proposed match. Adjibun later told me that he did not want his daughter to marry Nain because he was very distantly related to one of his enemies; Adjibun wondered whether he could trust his new son-in-law if there was ever a fight. Nevertheless the formal negotiations must be carried through; not to do so would be an insult to Nain's kinsmen (Tausug have fought over less). But Adjibun deliberately demanded a very high bridewealth which he knew Nain and his kin would not be able to raise.

The bridewealth, or *ungsud*, literally means "that which is given in payment." Ideally it is a transfer from the *usba* of the boy to the *usba* of the girl, although in practice all the close kindred—on both the father's side and the mother's side—of the boy contribute. Any kinsman of the girl can also demand some part of the bridewealth, although it is considered bad form to make a demand if one has not contributed in some way to the upbringing of the girl. The bridewealth has several constituent parts: some is used to pay for the expenses of the wedding feast and entertainment, some is used for the couple themselves, and a small part—often an animal—is technically a payment by the boy's *usba* for the rights to filiate (or join) any children born of the union to their group.

Adjibun made the following demands as the bridewealth of his daughter: 400 pesos to purchase gifts for the couple; 3 cows, 10 sacks of rice, 25 cartons of cigarettes, 8 boxes of matches, and the services of 4 professional xylophone players and singers, to be used at the feast; a water buffalo as payment for the rights in the children; a gold ring for the girl's mother; 50 rounds of carbine ammunition for Adjibun; 10 pesos for the *guru* who taught the girl to read the Koran; large frying pans for the girl's maternal aunt; a tray of food with a 5-peso flag attached for the girl's maternal grandmother; a *kris* (sword) for Adjibun; a *kris*, for the girl's uncle, and a flashlight for a friend of the father. The last demand was made because when the girl was born, Adjibun could not find his flashlight to fetch the midwife and borrowed one from a friend. He made a sacred promise that when the girl was married he would demand a new flashlight for his friend. The making of sacred promises to God in this manner in situations of stress is very common; if the situation turns out satisfactorily, the promise must be kept.

Marriage usually takes place shortly after the final agreement is reached on the bridewealth, as soon as the required property can be brought together. Occasionally prospective marriages are arranged between very young couples; in cases where the bride has not yet reached puberty, the marriage will be delayed until several months after menarche. Sometimes the groom will live in her house during the interim period and perform suitor service (gathering firewood, running errands, watching animals, and so forth) for her parents, although this is not always required.

On the day prior to the wedding, the groom's side delivers the entire bridewealth; any deviation from the formal demands is grounds to break off the engagement. Preparations for the marriage begin very early the next morning in both houses. Kinsmen, friends, and guests of the couple will gather during the morning at the respective houses. A cow or water buffalo will usually be slaughtered; there will be xylophone or gong music performed by professional musicians, with considerable merrymaking, conversation, and eating. Guests include not only the immediate kinsmen of the couple, but also distant political or military allies.

In the late afternoon the groom is carried, or rides by horse, to the house of the girl in a large procession consisting of all the guests who had previously assembled at his house, amid raucous yelling and shooting of guns. The marriage ceremony, consisting mainly of prayers in Arabic, takes place later in the evening. The girl is secluded during the entire affair; the ritual is conducted

between the boy, the girl's father, and the religious official. Following the ceremony, the groom is led to the bride. He symbolically touches her forehead, indicating his right to touch his wife. For the remainder of the night the couple
sit side by side without smiling or talking; it is considered unseemly to appear
to be too happy about marriage. They always begin married life together in
the girl's household, although they may later move to his parent's or build
a new home.

Tausug practice polygyny in the rare instances in which a man can
support more than one wife. Separate households are always maintained if the
co-wives are the same age, although if there is a major difference in age they
may live together. There are more unmarried women than men due to the
high male death rate from feuding. The greater female sex ratio is only partially
offset by polygyny; financial considerations weigh heavily against a man who
wants more than one wife unless he is a headman or otherwise wealthy.

While marriage through formal negotiation and payment of bridewealth
is the most prestigious mode of marriage, elopement and abduction are quite

*Woman dancing to gong music at a wedding.*

common. *Pagsaggau*, literally "capture," of women is a relatively quick and inexpensive way for a young man to obtain a wife. It reflects on his bravery and masculinity, and is actually regarded by the girl as a rather exciting form of marriage.

Naju abducted both his wives. When he was a boy he made a solemn promise that he would always abduct his wives; since he was a rather spoiled younger son, his parents agreed that they would support him. He said he abducted his first wife a week after he first decided he loved her. One day when she was alone at the waterhole he grabbed her and carried her to the headman's house. She screamed loudly—whatever her private feelings were, it is always necessary to put on a show of resisting—and her parents were visably upset. But the headman's house is considered a sanctuary in these matters; the authority for the marriage negotiations rests with him. According to the schedule of fines fixed by the sultan, the bridewealth for an abduction is 140 pesos plus an additional 50 pesos fine to "reduce the shame of the parents." Usually the headman also takes a percentage of the fine. In theory the girl has the right to refuse to marry her captor, but in practice this seldom happens. If a young man suspects she may be reluctant, he may take her into the forest before going to the headman and seduce her, making it difficult for her to refuse to marry him.

*Bride and groom. Except for the shoes and watch, the clothes are traditional Tausug dress.*

Naju abducted his second wife several months after divorcing his first. He decided he wanted a certain unmarried woman and invited several friends and female kinsmen to help in the abduction. He approached her on a trail, but she sensed his intentions and fled. She was accompanied by her cousin who was prevented from hacking Naju with his bolo by the timely intervention of one of the women. Another woman ran after the young lady and carried her to the headman's house. Fifty pesos were immediately sent to her parents to "hide the shame." They sent word that they wished a bridewealth of 500 pesos, one cow, and three sacks of rice. While this is more than the minimum standard specified in the law for an abduction, it was accepted. They were married two days later in the headman's home. All negotiations are in his hands; the function of the minimum standard bridewealth legitimized by the sultan is to give the headman a bargaining position to fall back against if the girl's parents prove to be uncooperative.

The gamelike quality of abductions—in spite of the seriousness with which they are viewed by the girl's parents and the real possibility of violence if the boy is caught before he can reach the headman's house—is illustrated by the rule whereby it is customary in some situations to deliver a piece of old heirloom brass to the parents of the girl. The boy's messenger must carefully place the object on their porch before they discover his presence; they have the right to "capture" him and demand the payment of a further fine of 25 pesos upon his release.

The line dividing an abduction from an elopement is very thin. In Tausug belief an abduction is due to the desire of the boy, while an elopment implies desire on the part of the girl. Most girls would rather be abducted than admit to elopement. But if the parents of the girl are seriously opposed to the marriage, it is better to announce it as an elopement, so that they will not be able to criticize the young man.

One afternoon I was visiting the beach when a considerable commotion developed with loud yelling and shooting. A daughter of Datu Sakilan was to be taken by boat to another part of the island to arrange a marriage with her first cousin there. A young man named Adja—who had secretly loved her for some time—announced that if the boat left, he would run amuck and begin shooting. The party retreated, and it was decided that if he wanted to marry the girl he would have to make arrangements in the proper way and pay a reasonable bridewealth. However, the girl was the daughter of a *datu* and the bridewealth was likely to be high. So Adja conspired to abduct her, and with a little help from his friends he grabbed her at a waterhole several days later. They hid in the forest until midnight and then fled to the headman's house, announcing they had eloped. While the headman knew she had probably been abducted and seduced, he sent word to the parents that their daughter had eloped; a marriage by abduction would be more difficult to arrange. Her parents were extremely upset upon hearing that she actually desired the marriage, calling her a flirt and a loose woman.

The standard payment for elopement with the daughter of a *datu* is considerably more than for a nontitled person, and Adja and his kinsmen had difficulty finding the money. After two days the girl apparently became discouraged and tried to escape from the headman's house. She was obviously ambivalent about the affair, caught between her love for Adja and her loyalty to her parents, who were very much opposed. Everyone immediately gave chase in a spirit of good fun, and she was soon dragged back again to the headman's house.

Finally the money was collected, and the wife of the headman went to see her parents. They insisted it was an abduction—which called for a higher bridewealth—while she held to the fiction that it was the girl's desire to elope. They still refused to accept the bridewealth, however, threatening to take the case to the sultan who always stands as a court of appeals. Whereupon Ajamuddin, a young military leader in Tubig Nangka, announced that as far as he was concerned the couple could go into the forest and live together without a formal marriage, and he would defend them if there was any trouble with her parents. The headman then announced that in his capacity as *sara* (law) he would negotiate with the girl's paternal grandfather. Normally it is necessary for approval to be given by the bride's father, but in his absence or inability almost any paternal kinsman may give approval. A compromise bridewealth was agreed upon, approval was finally given, and the couple was eventually married after almost a full week of negotiations, during which time they were living at the headman's house.

The function of the headman in these cases is to represent the law in the amicable settlement of disputes arising from marriage transactions. The couple usually go to the headman in their own home community, although in Tausug legal theory the law is uniform throughout the island and it is possible to go to any authorized headman. Several times during my stay in Tubig Nangka couples arrived from distant regions to stay with the headman as sanctuary while he arranged their marriage by bringing together the two respective kindreds.

## Divorce

The bond between husbands and wives, especially after the birth of a child, is extremely close in both ideal and fact. The strength of the relationship is related to the high emphasis which is placed upon the solidarity between father-in-law and son-in-law, a bond which is said to be second only to the bond between father and son.

It must be stressed that a low divorce rate does not necessarily indicate a high degree of happiness in marriage; rather, it may indicate a low level of expectation from marriage. While many couples have considerable affection toward each other, a marriage will usually only break up for the nonfulfillment of other more practical obligations than mere lack of affection: failure to support, quarreling over money, barrenness, excessive gambling, disagreement over treatment of children, refusal of the woman to accept a co-wife, and others.

One of the most common factors in marital quarreling is excessive gambling by the husband. Almost all men who regularly gamble will sooner or later quarrel with their wives over this issue. A typical pattern is for the wife to scold her husband, perhaps also hitting him. Sometimes he may strike her in return, and she will go running to the headman screaming that she wishes a divorce. Tausug regard divorce quite seriously. A primary role of the headman (or his wife) is to mediate marital disputes and "look for goodness" (karayawan). The husband will often be encouraged to swear on the Holy Koran to stop gambling; this usually satisfies his wife. Juljani, a man who lived near me in Tubig Nangka, quarreled with his wife many times over his gambling. Even when he won she was angry; once she tore up all his winnings in anger. Women dislike gambling because it squanders household resources, leads to stealing and fighting, and may result in the death of their husbands. Juljani once pawned his father's water buffalo to pay gambling debts, and when his wife heard about it, she went after him in the public market with a knife. She emphatically threatened to divorce him unless he swore on the Koran to stop gambling.

Another source of serious marital disputes is disagreement over the treatment of children. Fathers are said to be emotionally closer to their children than mothers; children are thought to have more love and respect for their fathers. Small children often sit with their fathers at public gatherings, and affection between them is considered natural. Mothers seem much less likely to publicly express affection for their children. A husband may argue with his wife if he feels that she has imposed too harsh a punishment on their child. Adda once became so angry with his wife because she whipped his child for a minor reason that he shot his gun at her. Although he just meant to frighten her, she ran to the headman screaming that her husband was going to kill her, demanding an immediate divorce. She was persuaded to return to Adda; he was nicer to her after the incident, although they continued to argue about the children.

The greatest range of rights in divorce lies with the husband. A divorce which is desired by the woman and opposed by the man usually requires the double return of certain parts of the bridewealth. Even then the husband may refuse the divorce, although in practice this seldom happens. One way in which a wife can force a divorce, however, is to swear on the Koran that she will no longer live with her husband. If he still insists on his rights, he will risk contaminating himself and his children with her curse. In general it may be observed that while the formal legal rights in divorce belong to the husband, the wife has a variety of informal means at her disposal which are effective in practice.

The quickest means of divorce for the husband is the Islamic device of the threefold repudiation of the wife, or talak, in which a man merely states three times in front of the headman that he divorces his wife. The property settlement is usually quite favorable to the woman, and such cases are relatively rare. A more common method of divorce is called *pagbugit*, literally "to discard something unwanted," in which it is necessary for the man to specify his reason. Usually an attempt will be made to reconcile the couple; if the divorce is unavoidable, the headman will issue a formal written statement of the divorce which is intended to protect the woman from charges of bigamy by her former husband if she wishes to remarry. In some cases the headman may merely agree to a separation without a legally binding divorce. This does not inconvenience the husband who can always remarry if he wishes; if the wife wishes to remarry, she will to go the *sara* (law) and obtain the statement upon payment of the necessary fees to the headman.

Let us examine in detail a single case of divorce litigation which also involved the murder of the wife's lover. Late one evening a young unmarried man named Nasirin was ambushed and shot to death by unknown assailants in a community near Tubig Nangka. No one saw the killing, although there were rumors and speculations about the identity of the murderer. Nasirin had actually been killed by Hasar for supposedly touching his wife several times, although there was some question whether they ever had sexual relations. Hasar's wife, Jahara, had a reputation for being a flirt, and it was rumored she was having an affair with Nasirin. Several days after the shooting, Hasar's mother came to the headman of Tubig Nangka to discuss the possibility of a divorce. The case had previously gone to the headman in their community, but he was unable to settle it amicably, so the case was taken to the higher headman of Tubig Nangka. The real reason for Hasar's desire for divorce was undoubtedly the flirtations of his wife, but he was unwilling to publicly acknowledge the real reason because it would have amounted to a confession of guilt of killing Nasirin. The ostensible reason for the divorce was that Hasar did not get along with his mother-in-law who was always scolding him. Since they were married only two years and had no children, they continued to live with the wife's parents. Hasar wanted to take his wife and live with his parents, but his mother-in-law refused. Although it is said that a woman should always go with her husband, if there are no children the parents of the wife continue to feel that they have superior rights over their daughter.

Settlement of the case could not be reached in Tubig Nangka; the case eventually reached the sultan's son in Jolo town. He expressed his desire to see the case adjusted without divorce and convinced the couple to return together. It was agreed that they should alternate between the two houses. Hasar kissed the hand of his mother-in-law in a request for forgiveness.

Two months later, Abdullah, the father of the murdered Nasirin, came to the headman of Tubig Nangka and announced that before his son died, he had named Hasar as the killer. Abdullah said he would swear on the Koran his son told him this. He had come to the headman to publicly announce— and presumably obtain some approval for—his desire to take revenge against Hasar. In Tausug customary law it is acceptable to kill a man who touches one's wife, provided the reason is immediately made public. However, the fact that

Hasar had attempted to hide his action made the case much more difficult to settle.

A series of hearings was held at the headman's house in an effort to mediate the case. The girl was summoned and asked to swear that she had actually been touched by Nasirin. She admitted that she had asked her husband to kill Nasirin (I doubt if she actually did so, but it was necessary to remove any suspicion of personal sexual wrongdoing on her part). The father of Hasar (Hasar was not present because of the real danger of violence if he publicly encountered Nasirin's father) said that his son had told him not to pay blood money to Abdullah to "cover his shame" because "my son also had shame when his wife was touched." But the headman reminded him that Hasar's shame was already erased when Nasirin was killed; the important thing was now to pacify Abdullah. Abdullah, however, demanded 1500 pesos in funeral expenses and stormed out of the hearing when Hasar's father countered with an offer of only 250 pesos blood money. Several weeks later when it became apparent to Abdullah that he did not have sufficient allies to take revenge against Hasar, he settled for 500 pesos. He probably knew that his son was wrong; if he had really felt his son had been innocently killed he probably would not have accepted any blood money, and would have sought revenge against all odds.

## The Household

There is no specific Tausug word for the nuclear family of parents and children; in fact there is a dearth of terms for specific groups of any kind.

The two most commonly occurring forms of the household are based either on a single nuclear family of parents and children or upon a group of parents and children, one married child and spouse, and one set of grandchildren. In technical jargon this is called a *stem family* to distinguish it from a fully extended family household where three generations live together with more than one set of grandchildren (that is, two or more married couples living with their parents). The fully extended family is very rare among the Tausug; when it occurs, it is always based on two married sisters with their parents and husbands. The reason for this is not hard to find: the household is preeminently a woman's domain, and sisters are better able to get along with each other than unrelated women brought in by a pair of brothers. In addition, households are often formed on the basis of two or more sisters who have been divorced, widowed, or remain unmarried. Several households in Tubig Nangka did not have any permanent male, although there were always brothers living nearby to help with heavy chores.

In arranged marriages the couple always initially live in the girl's household. The explicit rationale for this custom is that the parents of the girl have an obligation to teach their daughter how to be a wife and supervise her relationship with her new husband. Matrilocal residence is prescribed for at least a year or at least until a child is born because the girl will usually want to have her first child in the company of her own household. After the birth of the child the couple will either remain with the girl's parents (usually only if they are both from the same community), move to the boy's parents, or build a new house. The choice of eventual residence is made in terms of a number of practical criteria: availability of land, financial condition, relationships with in-laws, and the number of people in the household. Independent neolocal residence in their own house is the Tausug ideal, however.

A common cause of moving is friction between female in-laws over the conduct of the household or ownership of property. Public conflict between father-in-law and son-in-law is very rare and is always censured. On the other hand, a man may not get on with his wife's mother, especially if she interferes with marital conflicts on the side of her daughter. There is usually some underlying unhappiness behind every decision of a young couple to move and form their own household. Usual reasons include a desire to make economic decisions on their own; it is very hard to avoid lending money to other household members if they request it, and a couple may feel more financially independent by themselves. The basic reasons Tausug give for wanting to live in their own house are very much the same reasons Americans would give, although there is much more individual variation in interpersonal relations within the Tausug household. Some people get along very well with their in-laws and have no desire to leave; indeed some women are said to enjoy the company of their in-laws more than their own parents.

The couple will initially reside with the groom's parents only in cases of abduction where the bride's parents refuse to accept him, or in instances when the parents are closely related and live near each other. Independent neolocal residence will seldom occur immediately after marriage, for the permanence of the marriage, which is more certain after the birth of children, must be assured before the labor and investment in a house is made.

While all the major household types are to some extent alternative patterns available to individual choice, in another sense they may be regarded as different stages in a normal developmental cycle. In the beginning a young couple establishes a new household with their young children. Years later a son will marry and eventually bring his wife back to live in his household, provided excess land is available for him to farm at home. Grandchildren will be born, resulting in a three-generational household. Then an unmarried daughter will marry and bring her husband to live in the household. After further grandchildren are born, it will become apparent that the house is too small, or perhaps there will be interpersonal conflicts; at this point the daughter, husband, and grandchildren split and form their own independent household, beginninng the cycle anew. The initial parents will eventually die, and the household will pass to the son. Throughout the cycle additional members may be attached to the household in terms of kinship to the wife: unmarried sisters, divorced persons, and others without a household. The details of the developmental cycle will vary from family to family, but the basic patterns of fission and fusion of members to the household remain the same.

A typical stem family household is represented by the house of Isnang in

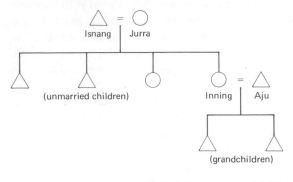

Figure 1. Isnang and his household.

*Typical stem family household (see diagram).*

Tubig Nangka (see the above photograph). Isnang, age 40, lives with his wife Jurra, their daughter Inning and her husband Aju, two unmarried sons and a daughter, and two male grandchildren. Isnang and Jurra are first cousins; their fathers were brothers. Inning and Aju are also related as third cousins on one side and second cousins on the other. They are a relatively wealthy household: Isnang has five cows and one water buffalo, while Aju owns three cows and two water buffalo. In addition they have two guns and a cash income from coconuts. Although two nuclear families living together have some moral obligation to assist each other financially, Isnang and Aju have separate household budgets, separate property, and separate rights to land. While the household cooks and eats together, there is some attempt made to keep account of who contributes to the provisions in an effort to insure an equitable division of expenses. The important fact about the Tausug household is that while there are strong moral sanctions for cooperation and solidarity among members, the household does not function as such in any legal sense. For example, it does not own property in common; even the house itself is individually owned by the head—in this case Isnang as the oldest male who was responsible for building it. Kitchen equipment, bedding, and furnishings are all individually owned.

Another household is represented by Samsurani, one of the religious leaders in Tubig Nangka. This household was in the process of splitting up because of interpersonal conflicts and the fact that there were 16 persons living in the one-room house. This is clearly too many; the average household has about 8 members, although the average size is increasing. Samsurani lives with his wife and 5 unmarried children, his married daughter and her husband, Aji, their baby daughter, his wife's sister's daughter, his wife's elder brother and his wife, and their 3 children. There were three nuclear families in Samsurani's household. His wife's elder brother was too poor to afford a house, so he moved in with Samsurani because there was excess land nearby to farm. Aji had been married to Samsurani's daughter for about 2 years. He gets on well with his wife, but has consistently quarreled with Samsurani about gambling. Once Samsurani scolded him for gambling and almost hit him. Aji argued back and became extremely angry. It was widely agreed that it was wrong of Samsurani to scold him for gambling; since Aji's wife did not object, it was none of his affair. But Samsurani told Aji to leave and take his daughter with him. At the time I left Tubig Nangka, Aji was constructing a new house on his father's land.

Another typical household is represented by Ajamuddin, the major military leader in Tubig Nangka. Aja (his nickname) lived with his wife and two daughters. His mother and father were dead, and his unmarried brother Suhaili sometimes slept in the house, alternating with other kinsmen. Aja's wife is his father's brother's daughter's daughter: technically his *anakun*, or niece. When they were first married, they lived for a while with the headman, his wife's paternal uncle, and then built their own house. Aja and his wife have quarreled many times, and she has threatened to divorce him after several serious arguments. They quarrel about the raising of the children and the fact that Aja is always going off to look for his enemies when his wife thinks he should be doing other things. While she occasionally hits him and once threw a rotten fish at him, he is reluctant to hit her because of his reputation as a brave fighter. "For a leader like Aja it is shameful to fight with women; if his enemies hear about it, they will just laugh and say that he can only fight with people weaker than he," my informant said.

# 3

# The Values of the Male:
# Bravery, Friendship, and Violence

THE WORD *violence* is one of those loaded English terms which must be carefully scrutinized if we are to use it sensibly with reference to other cultures. On one level of meaning it refers to an act of doing bodily harm to another with the intention of causing him injury or pain. The factor of intention is absolutely essential; without taking into account the meaning of the act we would be unable to distinguish on physical grounds alone between torture and a surgical operation. But a second—and very different—level of meaning is present when we speak of something as being violent when it represents the use of physical force beyond that which is usual or common in our culture. It is precisely this second level of meaning that causes the most difficulty when we try to apply it to the Tausug, for the everyday use of physical force on Jolo is so common that in spite of the condemnation of illegitimate physical force there is no Tausug word which can even approximately be translated as "violence." What is taken to be unalterable and part of the natural order is not singled out for special attention.

The use of physical violence in modern Western society is largely restricted to two major situations: "legitimate" force employed by the nation-state and "illegitimate" force employed by individuals. In both cases we do not believe that there is a human relationship between the perpetrator of violence and his victim: in the first instance because of the impersonality of the modern nation-state, in the second because more often than not we tend to classify violent individuals as psychologically aberrant or deluded. For the Tausug, on the other hand, violence is always a personal act directed against an enemy who is recognized as being an individual very much like himself, this fact alone makes it very different from the violence we are normally accustomed to.

Another problem in the discussion of violence stems from the fact that for a variety of historical reasons Western man has come increasingly since the

Renaissance to regard violent acts by individuals as very largely irrational. We normally do not think men would choose to be violent if they sat down and reasoned out their difficulties. I hope to show that this assumption simply does not apply to the Tausug: there is a rational dimension to their use of physical force which complements whatever passions may also motivate their conduct. In a culture where physical force is encountered at every turn it would be hard to imagine otherwise. Violence is often employed in legitimate self-help in defense of legal rights; power is diffused and the state is in no position to assert a monopoly over the use of violence. If each man must to some extent be his own policeman, then it makes no sense to think of violence as necessarily irrational.

The only Tausug word which has some of the connotations of the English word "violent" is *maisug*, literally "very masculine" or brave. A *maisug* person is combative and not deterred by physical danger and risk, one who has strong feelings and is not afraid to express them. While not all brave persons are necessarily hot-tempered (Tausug say hot-livered), extreme quickness to anger in a male presupposes the bravery necessary to sustain him in frequent violent encounters.

To be *maisug* is a kind of esthetic ideal with reference to a personal life-style; while violence may be morally wrong to the Tausug, it is still necessary to sustain that life-style. Public cowardice or a refusal to respond to an insult or affront is shameful in the extreme. An insult calls for retaliation; a death must be avenged. Even what might appear to be a relatively minor offense or insult may lead to a killing: an inappropriate remark about a defect in the other, a theft of a chicken, a contemptuous glance, an unpaid debt, or an accidental brush against a person in the marketplace. On one occasion two second cousins shot each other to death because one had sarcastically called the other by the English term "mister" which he interpreted as implying that he was uneducated (the term is used only for government schoolteachers). All violent acts hinge around the concept of *sipug*, or shame. The brave man must see that his shame is erased, not necessarily because it is morally good to do so, but because it is necessary to sustain his self-image as a brave man.

I want to stress the dual nature of the moral dimension to Tausug violence. In the secular common sense world a violent act is good only if it is justified by an offense which can legitimately be avenged; the Tausug say, when a man has been "victimized." The purposes of violence determine its good or evil character, not the fact of violence as such. In a religious context, on the other hand, vengeance and physical force are condemned as against the law of God. The distinction was made very clear to me in a discussion I once had with the headman of Tubig Nangka:

Ethnographer: So it is bad to take revenge, and it is also bad to be shamed. But unless a man takes revenge he will be shamed. So either way a man must be bad—if he takes revenge or if he does not?

Headman: True, but the sense of "bad" is different. If a man refused to take action when he has been shamed in front of others, he is bad in the sight of men present and men generally. But if he takes revenge he is bad in the sight of God. It is not possible to please both God and man at the same time. Murder is only justified in religion if it is clearly a case of retaliation for an unprovoked killing—everything else is condemned by God.

In short there are two basic levels to Tausug morality: a common-sense everyday morality and an ideal religious morality. While a comparable situation also prevailed in Medieval Europe, it is misleading to think of this distinction as hypocrisy in the modern sense of the word. It is not a question of the failure of one level of morality to adjust to the other (leading to a sense of the hypocritical when the two cannot be brought together); rather, it is a question of two opposed, but complementary, images of the source of power and the ideal personality: the power of God and the man of piety on the one hand, and the power of physical force and the man of violence on the other.

The fact that the morality of violence is alternatively approved on one level and condemned on another allows us to say in all fairness that while the Tausug are a violent people who believe in physical force, they are not a bellicose and warlike people. The hero is not the bully, but the man who "does what he has to do" when shame must be erased and honor restored. Children are not explicitly trained to express violence; on the contrary, parents make every effort to prevent children from fighting.

Furthermore, magnanimity is given great weight as a virtue. A man who refuses to be violent—so long as it is clear that he has the capacity and might normally be willing to do so—is not condemned. Rather it is thought that here is a man with a purer and more righteous set of values than his fellows. This became apparent to me when Karrun shot Isnani in the leg as he was farming. Karrun was an enemy of Isnani's half brother, but Isnani was trying not to involve himself in the trouble and even publicly announced that he would not support his brother. But Karrun shot him anyway, in a fit of rage. As I was bandaging the wound Isnani expressed dismay that Karrun had tried to kill him, saying that he bore him no grudge and would not attempt to kill him in turn. This refusal to take revenge was very unusual; everyone agreed that not one Tausug in 100 would have done the same. Yet Isnani's lack of anger was not interpreted as cowardice (there was no doubt of his bravery in other situations), but as virtue of a most pure sort.

In most contexts, however, the power of an enemy is to be overcome at any cost, never to be accepted or ignored. To admit publicly that one is angry at another person for a serious offense is to imply that one will try to take revenge. Vengeance always implies killing. According to the Tausug, killing is the most sensible form of retaliation, even if the original offense was not itself a killing, because if one merely does something mild to the enemy, he will in his turn still attempt to kill. The Tausug word for war or feud is *pagbunu,* which literally means "to fight with weapons." The word also means "to kill a person," or murder. The duality of these two concepts in a single word reflects the fact that serious conflict between males is not possible without attempting to kill, and that killing usually lends to a feud. The two ideas are almost inseparable in the Tausug mind.

Fights and quarrels between adult men have a marked tendency to move toward killing as their ultimate resolution. In a fist fight it is not uncommon to see the loser strike wildly at the air and yell (semiseriously) that he would kill the other if he could only obtain a weapon. Physical bravery is a basic value, the appearance of cowardice is very shameful, and a fight should go to the finish. To appear brave is an important value in the self-esteem of a man, and in some instances it takes precedence over basic values of kinship. I have witnessed occasions of friendly fist fights between kinsman which become deadly serious after a crowd gathered and the participants became sensitive to appearing cowardly before an audience. Playful fighting between both children and adults is rare for precisely this reason. A person mediating a feud must take into account the fact that the participants will not wish to appear too anxious for settlement in order to sustain the image of their bravery. In reality, cowardice seldom exists: to be Tausug is to be capable of fighting; a man must fight because he is Tausug.

## The Reasons for Conflict

In spite of the importance of shame and honor, it must not be thought that these are the only issues involved in Tausug conflict. Rather, the concept of shame is the key idiom in terms of which other more material interests are expressed and justified. A man who finds that his water buffalo has been stolen is likely to be upset at the material loss, but he is more likely to justify killing the thief in terms of his personal shame and honor.

The most common reason for wishing to kill another person is to take revenge for that person having killed a kinsman or friend. In all instances, however, the original killing will have been motivated by lesser causes; we will have to look more closely at the original precipitating factors in each instance.

One of the most common causes of violent conflict is theft. While theft in general is condemned, the theft of a small animal such as a chicken is considered more shameful to the thief than the theft of a large animal such as a water buffalo which always requires more bravery and risk and reflects favorably on the masculinity of the thief. In most instances it means a dangerous trip to a distant community where the thief has few kinsmen or allies; cattle theft between adjacent communities only occurs when there is a previous grudge between thief and victim. Pure cattle theft—that which is not premeditated by previous conflicts—is quite often an adolescent adventure in which the values of risk taking and bravery for their own sake take precedence over the actual material rewards. The risk involved is the danger of transporting the animal from its grazing pasture without being seen by the owner's kinsmen or neighbors. (Animals are easily recognized and are often branded today.) The finest coup, however, is to steal an animal at night from beneath the house of the owner; the risk is very great because if the owner's dogs bark, there is a strong possibility of being shot.

Immediately after World War II when guns were in ample supply but unequally distributed, there was a marked increase in cattle theft as men with firearms took advantage of those who were less well armed. As firearms became more equally distributed, the rate of cattle theft dropped abruptly—although it still remains a significant source of conflict. While small groups of young men will occasionally make a cattle-stealing foray into a distant region, it remains primarily an individual activity. There is no institutionalized raiding between communities or any other official sanction for cattle theft; on the contrary, theft is strongly condemned in a religious context. Community elders usually take a dim view of it, even if they were thieves when they were young. I remember discussing the issue with one old priest who was rather proud of his stealth as a cattle thief before he became a religious leader, although he was careful to point out that he would never do it now.

In addition to animals, other large items which may be stolen include boats, motors, and fishing nets. In the past, slaves belonging to one owner might be stolen for resale in some other island, although this practice stopped with the coming of American control. Theft of food or the clandestine harvesting of another's farm are extremely rare; they are thought to result in hak, a form of supernatural sanction in which the evil rebounds to the evildoer.

If the victim knows the identity of the thief, he may gather together his allies and attempt to take immediate revenge by killing. If he is caught in the act of theft the killing is legally justified provided it is a clear-cut theft and not merely an instance growing out of some previous conflict between the two. If the thief is discovered later, the victim may still attempt to take revenge, especially if he has allies and some military power, although the ideal is to "put the case before the law." The headman will summon the accused thief, and if he protests his innocence, he may be asked to swear on the Koran. If he refuses to swear or even refuses to appear, the headman may tell the victim, "It's up to you now," implying public sanction for his private revenge. In some instances the headman and his followers may join the victim in seeking revenge.

If the thief is not known and there is reason to suspect that he may be a person in the community, the headman may require that all adult males assemble at the mosque and swear that they did not take the animal. A person who did not take the oath would be presumed guilty and might be executed by the headman's armed followers. Because of possible repercussions according to Philippine law, public executions are rarer today than they were in the recent past—although one almost occurred in Tubig Nangka during my stay there—, and at present a refusal to swear would simply be taken as an admission of guilt, leading merely to a feud between the two alliance groups.

Sexual transgressions and petty jealousies may often result in serious conflicts or even killings. An incident occurred when Asmara and Arang were accused of having an affair together. An anonymous letter was put up in the mosque accusing the couple of "doing things like married people" and Balang, who was secretly in love with Arang, ambushed and killed Asmara out of jealousy and shame.

Men sometimes fight over the sexual honor of their female kin. While he was involved in some trouble in his mother's community, Pulunun and some of his allies were staying with Atari, an unmarried young man living with his first cousin in Tubig Nangka. One morning Pulunun learned that his cousin Atari had supposedly touched his sister and suggested that they have intercourse together. Pulunun was extremely upset, describing his feeling as one of *pangdada*, an extremely important Tausug concept meaning the resentment which is felt when one is betrayed by a trusted friend or kinsman. He was ashamed that someone should make an advance to his sister, even more so because Pulunun was currently helping Atari against his enemies. Fearing that Pulunun might attempt to kill him, Atari took refuge in the headman's house. The next morning Pulunun arrived in an intense fit of rage; he fired once over the house and was restrained from firing into the house only by the timely intervention of the headman's wife. Crying ambivalently, caught between his shame on the one hand and the fact that Atari was his kinsman on the other, he told the headman—who was extremely angry at Pulunun's attempt to challenge his authority—that he could kill him if he wished, as he did not want to live any longer. While everyone knew that Pulunun was wrong in trying to kill Atari, they sympathized with his predicament. Tausug believe that men are often drawn into tragic "trouble cases" by events not of their own choosing. One "finds" such a case; it was just Pulunun's luck to be put into a situation where he might have to kill his own relative. Ideally he should have immediately taken the grievance to the headman, who would have summoned Atari. But he knew that to seek a formal legal remedy he would forfeit his right to kill Atari; to take vengeance while a case is under adjudication is to risk making an enemy of the headman as well. Once Pulunun had quieted down, the case was amicably settled; after all, he did not really want to kill Atari, only to vindicate his shame. Atari was fined 50 pesos for the offense and the payment was given to Pulunun.

Men are occasionally killed by mistake, usually at night when it is difficult to recognize an approaching stranger. Because of fear of bad luck, Tausug will never give their own name when asked; a third party is always required. As a result two men who meet at night may be unable to identify each other unless a third person is present. If either is actively involved in a trouble case and is vigilant for his enemies, he may accidentally shoot the other thinking he is the enemy. If there was not reason to suspect enmity between the two men prior to the killing, the case might be settled by the payment of blood money, although quite often a feud may result with further killings.

Any public insult or affront to a person's self-esteem is likely to have violent consequences: insulting a person's honor or that of his kinsman, an ill-tempered remark, spreading malicious rumors about a man, or gambling arguments. Tausug come more quickly to anger than Americans do (or to love, for that matter). Quickness to anger is not subject to our kind of immediate intellectual inhibition in which we convince ourselves that the presumed object of anger is not "really" making us angry, and then proceed to dribble it away in reasoning.[1] While he might feel that the expression of anger was morally wrong in a particular situation, I cannot recall a single instance in which a Tausug would attempt to convince himself that the object of anger or fear before him was not real. The immediate impulse is to strike out against it, to face the object of anger with fear and resolution. For example, Tausug believe that the world is also populated by fearful ghosts called *lutau*, the partially decayed bodies of evil persons whose souls are on the way to hell. But fearful or not, the ideal way to face a *lutau* is to stand firm and fight; I was told many stories about men who shot at ghosts, wrestled with them, or hacked them.

While Tausug anger is usually a short madness, any immediate expression of rage or anger is likely to be offensive to others and may lead to a quarrel and potential killing. Like ourselves, the Tausug use the analogy of "heat" for anger. One speaks of an angry person as having a hot liver, but they take the metaphor much more literally than we, applying it to a greater range of situations. A child having a temper tantrum will have cold water thrown on him "to cool him off." Any potential disequilibrium in social relations is potentially "hot"—anger is the most conspicuous example—so that certain religious crimes are said to result in a drought or heat."

Many killings and threats of killings originate from a private sense of justice in which an individual provides the physical force necessary to redress his own grievance. Anthropologists usually refer to this system of private justice as *self-help*—a legal procedure which lies on the border between law and feud. While the headman has more raw power than the average man, there is no presumption that he should have a total monopoly of force within his community; rather it is assumed that each man will have to defend his own rights through violence from time to time. Isi, a young man who worked for me doing odd jobs, once borrowed 20 pesos against his salary to pay for a borrowed boat which he had wrecked off a reef while fishing. The owner told him that if he did not pay immediately there "would be trouble," implying that he would attempt to kill Isi, or at least seize some of his property. The only alternative he had from the threat was to go to the headman and claim that he was not responsible for the damaged boat, but there was no point in doing this because it was very clear that he owed the money. The boat owner, on the other hand, had no recourse against Isi except to threaten him with harm if he did not pay. It becomes very clear in cases such as this that the Tausug do not

---

[1] A superb discussion of this characteristic of our culture, especially among the university educated, is found in Paul Goodman's essay "On the Intellectual Inhibition of Grief and Anger," in his *Utopian Essays* (New York: Random House, 1951).

distinguish between civil torts (noncriminal breaches) and punishable crimes in the manner of Western law (although there is a distinction, which we will deal with later, between secular crimes and religious crimes). Any offense, including those that a Western lawyer would classify as a civil breach of contract, is potentially subject to violent sanctions through self-help by the victim.

Nonpayment of a debt may sometimes lead to a killing, for example, although only when the victim feels that he has been tricked or deceived so that his honor is at stake. Naju came to my house one afternoon to tell me that he could not repay a loan I had made him because he had not been fully paid for an animal he had sold to a man in a distant region. The debtor was a distant kinsman of the headman's wife, and she had guaranteed that the debt would be paid within two weeks after delivery of the animal. But after he failed to keep two appointments to pay the debt, Naju began to accuse the man of tricking him; as far as he was concerned the case meant killing. He was very angry when he came to see me, but when I tried to calm him he said that being a foreigner I did not understand that it is the *adat* of the Tausug to kill if one has been tricked. He was talking very loudly and angrily when another man (who was not involved in the case) came in and told him that it would be better not to look for conflict and just wait and think before doing anything rash. The headman's wife later paid Naju herself so that he would not make trouble.

In summary it may be said that any disagreement over the facts of a case in customary law may result in serious violence: breach of contract, failure of a guarantor to live up to his guarantee, disagreement over the respective shares in a joint business venture, ownership of animals or boats where more than one person has rights in the property, transactions involving firearms, or disagreements over the terms of the return of pawned property. In each of these instances, a person may feel that physical violence is necessary to defend his interests.

## Friends and Enemies

The defense of interests and the restoration of honor, however, cannot be accomplished alone. The individual must rely on help from his fellows, and he must be aware that his enemy will also have supporters. Friendship and enmity are the pivotal concepts in the social organization of Tausug violence; accordingly, it will be necessary to consider the way in which they talk about friends and enemies in everyday conversation.

The concept of friend (*bagay*) clearly derives its meaning from the fact that it is in opposition to enemy (*bantah*). When Tausug who have no friends outside their own community are asked why they have none, the usual answer is "Because I have no enemies." Actually accurate translation of the word *bagay* presents certain difficulties; while no other English term is suitable, "friend" is slightly misleading because we tend to think of friendship almost exclusively in terms of emotional solidarity devoid of any practical advantages. For the Tausug, however, friendship is valued precisely because it brings advantages: you help me and I will help you. The main, and usually explicit, reason for making friends seems to be the mutual help which each partner is able to anticipate—a dyadic contract of a sort. Yet, unlike other contractual relationships, friendship is conceived to be based upon the solidarity which only comes from strong sentiment; the ideal friend is one who is "like a kinsman" in conduct and reliability. There is also another sense in which the relationship between two friends is unlike a normal contract: the obligation to the friend is not legal, but moral—sanctioned by the highest religious and ritual foundations of the society.

One of the recurring themes in anthropology is to account for the presence of social cohesion in societies which are organized beyond the family and local community. Within the local group people interact in an idiom of sentiment which stems directly from constant face-to-face contact. But how to account for cohesion between relative strangers in a much larger society? Our own Western society has done so largely by erecting complicated networks of contracts and a civil law tradition which supports our complicated division of labor. Other societies have patterned social relations beyond the local group by extending the concept of blood kinship to include hundreds or even thousands of persons in complex ramified lineages. The Tausug have accomplished the same by extending the concept of friendship to create complex systems of alliance among persons who might otherwise remain relative strangers. While kinship is the foundation of the hamlet and local community, friendship is the cement which binds larger units together in the total society.

One important fact about friendship as a means of organizing people into groups deserves to be noted: friendship, unlike kinship, is an achieved social relationship which does not depend on the accident of birth. The Tausug assume an individual's participation in any acting social group is the result of his own conscious decision; a person can always change his friends, his alliances, or even his community if he wishes. The only exceptions are membership in the nuclear family, which is ascribed as a biological fact, and membership in the state (with its presumption of loyalty to the sultan) which is ascribed as a sacred obligation. Membership in all intermediate groups is always subject to individual choice, at least ideally, which is expressed in terms of a commitment to the group's leader.

The best way to discuss friendship and enmity in Tausug culture is to define in detail the meaning of the key terms which are used to describe those relationships, as well as certain associated terms. There are nine primary concepts in the domain of friendship: *bagay* (close friend), *bagay magtaymanghud* (ritual friend or "friend like a brother"), *bagay-bagay* (casual friend), *gapi* (ally), *bantah* (enemy), *tau hansipak* (opponent), *tindug* (retainer or follower), *bata'an* (bodyguard), and *tau ha ut* (neutral).

1. *Bagay* are a category of very close friends who will usually support a man in case of fighting, especially if their own interests are involved. Tausug deliberately attempt to create friends through ingratiation: offering to help a potential friend even though there is no obligation to help, inviting him to social occasions, offering gifts, and so forth. When men talk about the need to cultivate friendship in distant regions, they often compare the process to the creation of a "playground" so that the individual will have a "wide field to run in." It is said to be good for a man to have as many friends as possible in different areas so that he will be able to travel there in safety and may count on support in the event of trouble. In general, military leaders have the widest range of friendship contacts outside the community, while persons who are seldom involved in armed combat (either because of circumstances or personality) usually do not admit to having friends. Powerful headmen also have a wide range of friends spread throughout Jolo Island who can be counted upon to provide various kinds of assistance if needed. One way of cultivating friends is through the activity of "wandering about" in which armed young men in groups travel from place to place, looking for excitement, alliances, and women, staying with casual friends in order to renew old friendships and form new ones. The number of friends a man has outside his own community is usually directly proportional to the degree to which he is actively involved in armed conflict and feuding. Active alliance groups often attend cockfights in each other's communities, and these occasions are opportunities to extend the range even further.

The importance of friendship in insuring safety in travel was illustrated in Tubig Nangka when Ulanghutan, a young man from an adjacent community, decided to take some of his allies and launch a piracy raid against the Samal island of Parul, northeast of Jolo. They came to borrow the boat belonging to Ajamuddin in Tubig Nangka, but when he heard they were going to raid Parul, he convinced them not to go, saying he was a friend of the headman there. Some years before, Aja had run out of gasoline on the return trip from an expedition to buy guns in Basilan Island and stopped in Parul to refuel. The headman and Aja had become friends, and he felt he had to use his influence to prevent Ulanghutan from raiding Parul. Later the headman came to Tubig Nangka for a visit; he met the would-be pirates and they joked about the intended raid

2. *Bagay magtaymanghud* literally means "friends who are like brothers." It is a relationship of ritual friendship which is sanctified by swearing eternal loyalty and assistance on the Holy Koran. It is generally created between two individuals who desire to be friends, but may nevertheless have some reason to distrust the other and desire to cement the relationship with supernatural sanctions. Casual friends may decide on their own to become *bagay magtaymanghud*, or a legal official may arrange a swearing between two enemies in order to achieve an amicable relationship between them. In the latter case, however, the two have no obligation to mutually help each other, only to refrain from fighting. A typical instance of ritual friendship occurred when Akmad's wife refused

to allow him to marry the girl he had made pregnant. The parents of the girl threatened to kill him, and he was forced to flee. He went to a distant community to look for friends, formed an alliance with one man, and was taken into a household and given land to farm. After several months he became afraid that someone would kill him for his gun, so he suggested to some men in the community that they swear friendship together.

An oath is made by placing the right hand on the Koran and swearing to the conditions of the oath. A typical oath (in this case which ended a feud by creating a bond of ritual friendship between eight former enemies) is as follows, as repeated by the headman who administered it:

> You who will be brothers now place your hand on these thirty chapters of the Koran and promise now not to trick or betray each other. Whosoever will trick or betray will be cursed by the thirty chapters from the bottom to the top, by its letters and by its marks. However, if someone should say that you have betrayed the oath we will confer together to determine if it is true or not.

The eight then respond together: "It is accepted by God."

A person who breaks an oath is exposed to the dangers of a curse of unpredictable and terrible consequences, such as sickness, a horrible death, or other misfortune. The curse may follow a man into the afterlife or cause him to become a ghost. There was a certain notorious headman in Tubig Nangka during the American colonial period who killed perhaps 50 persons during his lifetime, including many persons with whom he had sworn friendship. He was considered very brave, but when he died it was widely believed that he became a ghost. Persons often decline to swear friendship when asked, saying that the risk of curse is too great, and suggest that the friendship be marked merely by a verbal promise. One man put the predicament very clearly: "If you swear with a man and then he kills your brother, you should just do nothing . . . but if you cannot control yourself and take revenge against your brother's killer then you will have a curse—that is why it is so hard to swear."

*Bagay magtaymanghud* have strong obligations to assist each other in fighting if they are able to do so, to assist with debts, to loan guns if needed, and to provide shelter and food. The oath is basically a dyadic relationship between two individuals. Even if a large group swears together it is conceptualized as a series of relationships between individuals, not a single unitary relationship of solidarity in the group as a whole. As a result, to kill a ritual friend's brother—as in the example above—does not destroy the relationship (at least not ideally) because the original pact was only between the two original partners.

3. *Bagay-bagay* are a category of very casual friends who may sometimes support a man in fighting but who generally cannot be relied upon. The doubling of the word in this instance—as in many Pihilippine languages—implies the notion of pretending or feigning; the term literally means "make-believe friends."

In fact, *bagay-bagay* are regarded as being just one step away from enemies; as one man put it:

> Before we decided to move here I went to see Jamah and asked him if he would kill me if I did. We were formally allied against each other. The case was settled, but I was never able to talk to Jamah personally about it. So I was afraid he might still want to kill me. But he said that his liver had cooled off (was no longer angry). . . . well, if he will not kill me, that makes us *bagay-bagay*.

*Bagay-bagay* do not include people met on the road or other transitory contacts. They are rather those people known well enough to have a friendly conversation, but who are not *bagay*. They often come to large ritual gatherings at a friend's house, but are seldom invited individually to eat, unless they happen to be in the house at the time food is served. In effect, they are all those people who are neither close friends, enemies, nor merely transitory contacts.

4. The term *gapi* or ally is usually used to refer to a category of persons with whom a man is allied in a given battle or trouble case not because of a primary relationship of friendship or kinship but because of a common mutual friend; "friend of a friend" might be a reasonable translation of the word. In very large battles persons who have never before known each other may be thrown together in an alliance because of the particular manner in which the alliance configuration crystalized in that instance. While they are not friends —although they may easily become so—they are still considered to be *gapi*.

5. *Tau hansipak* ("people on the other side") are a category of persons with whom a man is fighting or actively hostile either because they are allied with his personal enemies, or because he is allied with their personal enemies. One does not have a direct grudge against *tau hansipak*, other than the fact that they are supporting personal enemies. If two *tau hansipak* accidentally meet (a rather common situation), they often will not fight, unless one or both of their personal enemies are also present. Nevertheless, a man is always on his guard in the presence of *tau hansipak*. On one occasion I witnessed two rival groups who stood in this relationship accidentally meet in a mosque. Each group was conscious of the other, deliberately raising their guns where they could be seen and conspicuously releasing the safety locks. The priest nervously continued the ceremony until one of the groups left.

6. *Bantah* are a category of personal enemies who are allied against a man not because of an accidental configuration of the alliance system but because one has a case (*parakala*) against them, often a person who is held responsible for killing a kinsman or friend. A *bantah* is by definition a person who will kill one if given the chance; it implies extremely negative feelings such as hatred, anger, and the like.

But the relationship between enemies is more than merely a set of psychological characteristics; it is also a fundamental legal category so that persons who are *bantah* to each other are entitled to have this fact recognized. The primary purpose behind mediation of disputes is to end the relationship between enemies. Enemies remained opposed until such time as legal processes of mediation have ended the relationship (or until the hostility ends by default of the weaker party and is accepted by the stronger), in rare instances for many years.

Enemies may be classified as either active or inactive, depending on whether the relationship is subject to constant concerns and immediate attention. A man's most recently acquired enemies will generally be treated as the most active and dangerous. Inactive enemies tend to be those who live in very distant regions, or those with whom a formal settlement has never been reached, even though overt hostility has stopped.

7. *Tau ha ut* ("people in the middle") are neutrals who are not involved in a case for any of several reasons. They may have kinsmen or friends on both sides, be persons without access to firearms, or be religious officials, who are to some extent outside the friendship and alliance system. They may be the insane, the lame or the sick, or individuals who for a variety of personal reasons simply do not wish to fight and have made this intention public. Such persons are seldom condemned, unless they refuse to support a very close relative. Women, the elderly, and children are always neutrals in any conflict; violence against them is severely censured, although they are sometimes hit by accident.

8. *Tindug* refer to followers, whether one has sworn friendship with them or not. In Tausug theory, all people in the community are *tindug* of the headman; all Tausug, *tindug* of the sultan; all Moslems, *tindug* of God, and so on. *Tindug* should be friends of their leader, or at least friends of friends. Leaders sometimes attempt to convince others that they have more followers than they really do. One man expressed this idea in the following manner:

> If you have many friends you should try to get them to accompany you to distant places. The people there will respect you and say that you must have many *tindug*, and they will be careful before involving themselves in cases with you. Sometimes you can get people to come along who are not your friends, and then people will say you have more *tindug* than you really have. Everyone admires a man who has many followers. If you come to a feast with many followers and guns, people will respect you and immediately offer you cigarettes and betel. For this reason it is good to have as many armed men as possible with you when you go traveling.

9. *Bata'an* are followers who serve as bodyguards. A Tausug headman or leader of any social standing seldom travels outside his home community to a social event in another community without the presence of a number of bodyguards, usually younger men, both to impress people with his status and personal power and to protect him against the possibility of violence. Traditionally, bodyguards carried the spears and betelbox of the leader; today they may carry guns, while the leader himself may only wear a pistol or bladed weapon.

Tausug distinguish very clearly between kinship and friendship; a person is not normally considered to be both a kinsman and a friend at the same time, although this may actually be the case. In reference to military activity, however, the distinction between friends and enemies is primary; kinsmen may be considered *de facto* friends in the sense of guaranteed support in the event of trouble. When a Tausug says, "All my kinsmen in this community are also my friends," he is really implying, "All my kinsmen in this community can be counted upon in the event of a fight." However, the kinship sanction is generally considered to be stronger than friendship. As one young man put it talking about a certain friend: "He is much more than a friend to me, he is also my kinsman" (thus reversing the way most Americans would put it). Kinship is much more likely to be emphasized if the men live together in the same community; distantly related men in different communities might refer to each other as friends rather than relatives.

Thus, the essence of friendship between two Tausug is a certain style of reciprocity, especially in relation to violent conflict: you help me and I will help you. (Remember, however, that it is not a contract but a *moral* relationship.) Now there is a very interesting characteristic of mutual gift giving (even though the gift is a service) between men which bears on the problem of violence in Tausug society: usually the level and intensity of reciprocity can be increased much more easily than it can be decreased. It is possible to do more for the friend than he did for you, thus increasing his obligations when he reciprocates, but it is very difficult to do less; to break the chain of gift giving is not to go back to the earliest stages of the relationship, but to catapult it into hostility itself. In short, there is considerable fluidity and movement between these recognized categories with increasing levels of friendship or enmity. One can become more *of a friend* or *more of an enemy*, but one cannot decrease the level of friendship or enmity in a similar steplike manner. Only a total reversal of the relationship is possible. As a result alliances are very unstable, and today's friend may become tomorrow's enemy.

## Reciprocity, Revenge, and Shame

Reciprocal gift giving involving commodities, services, and sentiments[1] is pervasive in Tausug social organization. Two major forms of reciprocity may be identified: quasicontractual reciprocity and a type of reciprocity called *buddi* which may be freely translated as "debt of gratitude." Quasicontractual responsibility involves fairly accurate keeping of accounts of the mutual debts and is illustrated in the mutual monetary exchanges which take place at every formal social affair, as well as cooperative labor exchanges during planting and harvesting. *Buddi*, on the other hand, involves very nebulous record keeping in

---

[1] While we do not normally think of sentiments being exchanged in the manner of gifts, a little reflection will convince one that this is so. Even with the exchange of gifts, the idea that "it is the thought which counts" illustrates the fact that the sentiment is at least as important as the gift itself.

which there is no precise agreement on the terms of repayment precisely because the things exchanged can never be strictly equated with each other in any rational manner. It is very difficult, for example, to determine how much monetary assistance is equivalent to a given amount of political support or military aid. As a result, each man will attempt to insure that the debt of gratitude is fully paid by deliberately paying more than might be thought necessary, thus increasing the obligation further in his partner in an ever increasing spiral of reciprocity.

*Buddi* is often defined in general terms as "love repaid by love," or more specifically as "a debt which cannot be demanded." It is originally created in a person who was the recipient of a great favor which was not requested or expected. He feels a strong moral obligation to do something in turn for his friend, and it is his responsibility to determine the most appropriate time for repayment. A man would never demand repayment of a debt of gratitude except in extreme anger, although he might relay his need to the other through a third party. If the debt of gratitude is not spontaneously repaid when needed, a man is said to be overwhelmed by the sentiment of *pangdada*, a feeling of rejection and hurt feelings which among the Tausug easily turns to rage and anger. The defaulting debtor would be described as a person "without shame" if he were deliberately shirking his responsibilities. If he were merely unable to repay the debt, he would have a feeling of *luman* to the debtor, another term which has no exact English equivalent, but may be rendered as "feeling of social distance in a situation where there is potential shame." Four key terms are therefore crucial in understanding the dynamics of reciprocity in Tausug armed combat: *buddi* (gratitude), *sipug* (shame), *pangdada* (resentment), and *luman* (deference or social distance).

A typical example of a debt of gratitude in fighting occurred when Ajamuddin and a group of his followers went by boat to Basilan Island to raid a wealthy community of Christians and Chinese which was said to be undefended. The mission was unsuccessful; they encountered some Philippine government soldiers and were prevented from reaching the town, although they did kill one of the soldiers. Their boat was wrecked and they were unable to return to Jolo. While they were in this desperate condition and being pursued by government troops, they were befriended by a group of coastal dwelling Tausug who supplied them with a boat and enabled them to return. The debt of gratitude for this act of kindness lay dormant for nearly two years, until the Basilan people needed help in a feud of their own. Ajamuddin and his followers returned to Basilan and assisted their friends in fighting on no less than four occasions. Furthermore, this reciprocation built up a further debt of *buddi* in the Basilan group who traveled to Jolo several times to assist Aja in fighting there.

To go voluntarily to the aid of another in battle, or to assist in taking revenge when one does not have a clear obligation to do so, builds up a debt of gratitude in the other which must be reciprocated; this debt assumes enormous proportions if the assistor suffers a loss in battle. If a man was killed while helping a friend in fighting, the friend would feel a huge debt to repay the dead man's kinsmen for the loss by taking responsibility for seeking revenge. In practice, fighting debts are expressed as obligations between military leaders, and the commitment of the leader implies participation of his followers. Technically, however, debts of gratitude exist only between individuals, never between whole groups.

Military assistance is often given in a deliberate attempt at ingratiation in which one party, especially when involved in a feud, anticipates help in return. In addition assistance is sometimes given by a group which finds itself accidentally caught in a situation when fighting starts. If a man is traveling with another man who encounters his enemies, he will usually assist his companion in fighting simply because to run in face-to-face situations of combat is considered shameful and casts doubt on the masculinity of those who refuse.

Reciprocity is expected only if the partner is in a position to give assistance. A person or his alliance group may remain neutral if there is an acceptable reason for doing so, such as a lack of weapons or ammunition, but in many cases the obligations are strong enough that the person will be expected to borrow or buy the necessary arms if he has the means. The lending of guns also figures importantly in military reciprocity. Since not everyone owns a gun, an elaborate system of temporary borrowing of firearms among kinsmen and close friends has developed; whenever a major feud threatens the peace of a region, this system allows a considerable number of weapons to be brought in from surrounding communities which are not currently involved in difficulties of their own. There are two major kinds of gun exchange: borrowing within the community among kith and kin, and intercommunity borrowing between friends and distant kinsmen. Loans of guns to casual friends are seldom made because the risk of betrayal is too high; firearms represent the major capital investment of most rural households.

Reciprocity and the exchange of fighting debts between military leaders from different communities is the mechanism by which large fighting forces—sometimes several hundred armed men—are put together. Thus, even though the immediate moral obligation to avenge a death or redress a grievance may rest only with a single individual, or at most his very close kinsmen, Tausug are able to construct large military alliances based upon friendship which go far beyond the bounds of the effective kinship group.

The pervasiveness of the sentiment of reciprocity in Tausug culture is further understood when we consider the importance of the value attached to vengeance, which is, after all, merely a special form of negative reciprocity in which men exchange hostile feelings that drive them apart instead of bringing them together. While *buddi* is described as a debt which must be repaid but cannot be demanded, a blood debt calling for vengeance would have to be described as "a debt which must be demanded, but cannot be repaid." Tausug sometimes talk about a "debt of a soul" in this context; the killer must pay with his own soul. We might say that in addition to useful goods, services, and sentiments, Tausug also exchange funerals.

The term for revenge is *mamauli*, which also means the act of repairing or fixing something which must be corrected, a state of disequilibrium which must be corrected. But retaliation against an enemy usually drives at going beyond mere equivalence. One repays the blood debt not only to discharge the debt, but also to shift the obligation to the enemy. A man typically does more in retaliation to his enemy than he did originally, so as to further draw out the hatred of his kinsmen or allies. One tries to provoke the enemy by a particularly outrageous act so that he will attempt to reciprocate and continue the feud. Just as it is always easier to increase the intensity of feeling of gratitude than to decrease it, so it is also easier for feelings of hostility to mount endlessly until external legal pressures are brought to bear to end the feud.

Refusal to honor a debt of gratitude to one's military allies or friends, or refusal to demand a repayment of a blood debt from one's enemies opens the individual to the charge of being "without shame" (*way sipug*). These two uses of the word point to two complementary dimensions of the concept of shame: shame as "dishonor" and shame as the capacity of the virtuous man. Shame is being aware of the self in relation to society. It must be noted in this regard that shame is always the property of individuals; it never resides in kinship groups, families, or communities.

Furthermore, the concept of shame is not only used to describe an inner feeling, but it is also used as an ideal which serves to justify the individual's enmity. To say "I was shamed by so-and-so" is an attempt to justify relations of enmity with him. By verbally identifying himself as an embarrassed person in a situation where he has been insulted, a man is saying that while he may not have been able to honorably sustain himself in that particular occasion, he is properly disturbed by the fact and may prove worthy on another occasion. For a man to say that he has been shamed is to say not only what he is, but also what he will be.

The basic element in shame is the discrediting of the self in front of others. The idea of bravery and masculinity is a major facet of an adult male's image of himself. If an offense is committed against a man, the shame he feels arises from this reduced self-image before the eyes of people in general and particularly before the enemy himself. To be unwilling to take revenge or engage in a fight with the enemy disturbs the defined expectation of normal relations between enemies. The need to avoid the shame of seeming to be unwilling to fight back in some instances is more important than whether the revenge is actually successful. One of the most usual statements for litigants in a legal proceeding to say is "We know we will have to accept settlement sooner or later, but give us another chance to fight first, then come back and try to settle us." It is this value which is powerfully expressed in the Tausug saying, "The thing which kills a man is embarrassment."

The importance of shame in not appearing too cowardly is seen very clearly in those rare instances in which two enemies meet face to face but are unable to fight because they are restrained by the situation. In such instances a man may literally cry from shame, while his enemy sits opposite him and "swallows him with his eyes." I was present in a coastal market one afternoon when a young man named Rasid arrived only to discover the presence of another man who had killed his first cousin several months before. His first reaction was to release the safety lock on his gun, but he was restrained by his companions who did not want to offend the headman in charge of the market who was responsible for preserving the peace. The headman sensed the situation and called the leaders over for a conference. Although Rasid agreed there should be no trouble in the market out of deference to the headman, he was almost crying. His eyes were red, and he attempted to turn his face from me several times. People commented that it was a very difficult situation for him; he was caught between his shame before his enemy, and his deference to the headman. Hasim, the enemy, returned after Rasid had left the market. He was quite proud of himself, having forced his enemy to sustain a sense of shame; extremely brave men deliberately attempt to put their enemies in this kind of situation.

## An Instance of Shame

A more entangled situation of the same kind which illustrates some of the major elements of the value of *sipug* occurred in Tubig Nangka. One of Ajamuddin's kinsmen was to be engaged to a girl who lived in Ulanghutan's compound in an adjacent community, and a time was set for the formal negotiation of the marriage. Ajamuddin and his followers were at that time allied with a military leader from the other side of the island, Isnin, who had a friend named Asad who was a staunch enemy of Ulanghutan. Ajamuddin felt that the occasion would be a good time to arrange a settlement between the two enemies, inasmuch as there would be many people present and Ulanghutan would not be in a position to refuse. So he told Isnin to bring his friend Asad along for a confrontation with Ulanghutan. While Ajamuddin knew that Ulanghutan would be upset to see his enemy face to face, he hopefully anticipated that Ulanghutan would behave reasonably out of deference (*luman*) to him. He failed to inform Ulanghutan that his enemy would be arriving.

A group of over 100 people assembled, including all the kinsmen of the boy to be engaged, Asad, Isnin, Ajamuddin, and their respective followers, numbering about 25 guns. Asad, however, was unarmed to avoid any suggestion of possible malice and was instead carrying one of the numerous trays of food and gifts. When the group approached the compound Ulanghutan's young son saw his father's enemy and ran to warn him. Ulanghutan came out of his house in a rage, fired wildly into the air several times, pointed his gun at Ajamuddin and screamed, "You know Asad is my enemy—why do you bring him here to cause me embarrassment?"

All the armed men retired a short way down the path. Ulanghutan sent a runner to request help from his allies as he felt outnumbered. People were screaming that all the unarmed people should go home because there would surely be a battle. The marriage negotiations proceeded very quickly under great tension while Asad, Ajamuddin, Isnin, and all their armed followers waited in a nearby orchard for the unarmed crowd to disperse before deciding what action to take. People were saying that Ajamuddin would certainly fight with his distant kinsman Ulanghutan before the sun set.

The problem was that nearly everyone was shamed before nearly everyone else. Ulanghutan was shamed by Ajamuddin before his enemy Asad and his own companions. He said, "Aja has no respect for me; he brings my enemies here to swallow me with their eyes," implying that Asad would just sit and stare at him and he would not be able to react.

Ajamuddin, on the other hand, felt that he had been shamed by his kinsman and friend Ulanghutan, saying that his behavior in pointing the gun at him indicated a lack of deference and respect in their relationship. He felt that his friends Isnin and Asa would feel that he did not really have any influence with Ulanghutan; he was shamed before Asad for having invited him to come along under such humiliating circumstances.

Asad was the most shamed person of all. Ulanghutan's behavior was a direct affront to him and being unarmed he was not in a position to immediately react. He was ashamed to the others present because he felt that they might fight because of him. Asad had come to apologize to Ulanghutan, but his apparent refusal to accept the apology only increased his shame, for to continue to offer to apologize under the circumstances would certainly have indicated gross lack of self-respect.

Isnin was probably shamed before all those present, at least a more hotheaded man would have been shamed. But Isnin is a very level-headed young man—although extremely brave—and he refused to discuss the incident with the others in terms of his personal shame. Ajamuddin later told me that if Isnin had said he was ashamed, there would have been no possibility of avoiding a battle. He said that "the shame of Isnin would have increased my own shame and we would have fought with Ulanghutan."

This incident almost resulted in a very unusual battle, with close kinsmen fighting on opposite sides. It was settled only after I was sent back to Tubig Nangka in my jeep to bring the headman who later convinced the armed men to go home. Subsequent mediation resolved the difficulty, and Asad was eventually settled with Ulanghutan. The incident illustrates that it is possible for serious conflict to develop in some instances even though the issues involved are very minor; a battle almost occurred solely because of the issues of shame and honor. The alliances which would have crystallized would have forced Ajamuddin to fight against his own kinsmen, and there was general condemnation of Asad for having created such a situation. One young man told me that if a battle started he would have tried to shoot Asad in the back, even though he would be supporting Ajamuddin against Ulanghutan. Actually, Ajamuddin knew that it was his fault for failing to inform Ulanghutan as a courtesy that he was bringing Asad, but as he later told me, "It is our practice to fight even if it is our fault—when we are embarrassed, we have to fight."

## Alliances and Feuds

When Tausug talk about alliance groups of young men who fight together they very rarely refer to the group as a whole. In fact there is no commonly accepted term to refer to an alliance group, in spite of their overwhelming importance in Tausug society, although occasionally the phrase "one group who help each other" is used. It is more common to refer to a group by the name of its leader, as in the phrase "Hamid will help in fighting" in which it is implied that Hamid will not come alone, but will be accompanied by an unspecified number of followers.

The alliance group is both leader-centered and situation-centered. The size of the group for any particular activity will depend both upon the situation itself and upon the leader's ability to mobilize his followers. In any community, younger men who engage in fighting may be divided somewhat arbitrarily into four categories. First, there are those military leaders who actively seek alliances outside the community and may lead fighting in distant districts. Second, there are the regular followers of these leaders. Third, there are those who do not normally involve themselves in fighting, but may do so if their own interests are directly involved. Lastly, there are the weak and the socially irresponsible. In general, those more likely to be involved in fighting have more outgoing and self-assured personalities. They are better speakers and are more highly skilled in the use of rhetorical language. They are usually more intelligent and more introspective and deliberate in their conduct.

Since the alliance group is defined in terms of its leaders, it does not necessarily have any permanence beyond the life of the leader. Technically, leadership in Tausug alliance groups is not based upon traditional authority in which the defined status and role of the authority is paramount, but rather upon charismatic authority in which the leader largely defines his own position by the sheer force of his own personality. As a result, with the decline of the influence of any particular leader, the following which crystallized around him may also disappear. It may actually be more accurate not to talk about "groups" at all, but rather "networks" in which each man is connected to every other by a complicated chain of personal ties. The Tausug pattern of structuring political and military life in terms of temporary factions rather than of stable political groups, is typical of the Philippines, both in pre-Hispanic times and in the present. Political groups as such are rather unstable; the more enduring units are the various dyads composed of two men who have formed an alliance based on friendship. A slight change in a few key dyads may completely change the configuration of the "group" as a whole, somewhat like shifting carbon atoms in organic chemistry.

The only alliance groups which show long stability are those based on kinship and friendship and which are localized in a single community, or more rarely in adjacent communities. These can be called *minimal alliance groups* because they are the smallest localized units for purposes of conducting military activity. The size ranges from about 10 armed men to as many as 25, although the size will always vary with the situation at hand. For example, several men may drop out of a particular feud because their wives are related to people on the other side and they do not wish to court domestic difficulty as well. The number may increase if the issue at stake is a particularly heinous moral outrage.

It is clearly to a man's advantage to be a member of a minimal alliance group. An individual who does not support his fellows may be forced to seek revenge against his own enemies alone or in the company of only a few very close kinsmen. But a man does not specifically set out to join an alliance group as such; rather, he attempts to activate a specific alliance with one of the existing members—usually the leader—which will bring him into the network of the group.

In addition to support for its members in feuding, the activities of the minimal alliance group also include the mutual lending of guns, economic help in the purchase of guns and ammunition, the protection of the community, and support for the legal functions of the headman. While they often act in pursuit of merely "private" interests, they also provide the threat of violence which is necessary for an effective headman to perform his public legal functions.

While simple feuds are often conducted between small groups of opposing men in minimal alliance groups, more complicated feuds and larger battles are occasionally fought between *medial alliances* consisting of a union of these minimal groups. Within the medial alliance the constituent minimal alliance

*Minimal alliance group.*

groups do not lose their separate identities, but retain identification with their respective leaders. Any given battle, either defensive or offensive, is organized by the leader in the community which "owns" the case and has primary responsibility for the redress of the grievance. He enlists the help of leaders from other communities with whom he has active friendship; they in turn bring their friends, and so on, in ever more complicated ramified ties of friendship. Medial alliances are not necessarily located in a particular region but may involve groups from very distant parts of the island. This fact is extremely important in Tausug political organization because it signifies that conflict does not involve permanent rifts between territorial units; rather, it occurs between alliance groups which are composed of persons widely separated in space. Every Tausug leader has a number of friends in distant communities who will assist him in the event of trouble. The leader and "owner of the case" is obligated to provide for the cost of hospitality required when military allies come to help. These expenses can be considerable; a group of 100 allies in a medial alliance group can consume one sack of rice a day, in addition to large quantities of cigarettes, coffee, and fish.

Medial alliances are extremely unstable; it is not uncommon for two groups to fight on one side at one time and the opposite side two months later. The reason for this lack of stability stems from the individualism and lack of group orientation which allows each individual to reconsider his participation in the alliance with each new development. There is a kind of "domino effect" in alliances in which a slight shift in the nature of the relationship between two leaders will force all others to reevaluate their own involvement. For example, the entire alliance configuration in the region around Tubig Nangka shifted rather dramatically within two weeks as a consequence of a fight between two former allies who argued during a gambling session. Former allies became enemies, and former enemies became friends as each leader reconsidered his own position in relation to what the others were doing.

While these shifts in alliance structure are very common, they do not occur in a self-consciously cynical and Machiavellian manner. A cynical betrayal of a friend is unusual; Tausug very rarely swear friendship knowing that they intend to break the pact. When betrayals occur, they are usually because a man is forced to make a decision between two friends or between a friend and a kinsman. A man's involvement with a case and the alliances he may forge in order to deal with it are thought to be a part of his fate or luck. He is usually more concerned with coming to terms with the existing configuration of alliances than with plotting to manipulate long-range changes.

Former enemies are often brought together in peace as a result of the emergence of a third common enemy shared between them. Antagonism between two large medial groups—which in some instances may number hundreds of participants—often tends to be stalemated within six months to a year after the outbreak of hostilities, usually because they have in the meantime acquired more immediate trouble cases to deal with. The motive for settling an old grudge is often precisely because a new one takes precedence and long-term fighting on the level of the medial alliance would very quickly result in a war of all against all. Thus, over a several-year period in any region many of the minimal alliance groups will have engaged in fighting with many of the other groups in the same region, although at any given time former enemies may be friends.

The antagonism between two large alliances is usually based upon more than one trouble case or issue between them. Each minimal alliance group in the confederation has its own very particular reason for being there: one may be fighting to avenge the death of a kinsman, another to assist a friend of the leader, another to redress an instance of cattle theft, and so on. Mediation between large alliances is often difficult because of the large number of trouble cases which separate them. It is considered very shameful for one member of an alliance to settle his own particular case with his enemies and then withdraw from the alliance, leaving his allies to continue the fight alone. Ideally all the issues separating the two alliances must be solved at the same time.

In the past it was common for leaders of medial alliance groups—usually influential regional headmen or military leaders—to cement alliances with other regionally influential headmen to form a *maximal alliance*, numbering perhaps as many as a thousand armed men. These alliances operated primarily in cases of extremely large feuds between headmen, and in the wars of succession for the sultanate; they no longer exist in traditional form at present. Maximal alliances today are largely conducted within the framework of Philippine electoral politics and use ballots as much as bullets.

The Tausug concept of the feud is embodied in the term *parakala*, or "trouble case." Faced with a case which calls for action on his part to avenge a grievance, a man will either attempt to act by himself if possible or enlist the help of friends and allies, including the kinsmen in his minimal alliance group. If he has friends in other communities, he may also enlist their assistance in the form of a medial alliance. The number of people involved in a conflict will naturally vary in each instance with the range of alliances of those persons who are primarily responsible for organizing it; the more powerful the leader, the larger the feud which is likely to result from his involvement. In addition, the power of the legal authorities in the region will also influence the intensity of the conflict; the weaker the authorities, the more protracted a feud is likely to become. Furthermore, there are powerful ethical factors which influence the organization of feuds. A man who is clearly in the wrong is likely to have more difficulty recruiting assistance in his case, even among those who might normally be expected to help him.

The intensity of a feud is also influenced by the nature of the relationship between the antagonists. For example, a killing within the minimal alliance group located in a single community is not likely to result in an extended feud with multiple acts of homicide. Usually, the case is quickly settled by the payment of blood money to the victim's relatives or perhaps a single act of retaliation. If the killer and his victim come from adjacent communities a simple feud may result with multiple acts of homicide. Small groups will penetrate each other's communities and set up simple ambushes. The avenger, however, is highly selective in his choice of victim; he is usually looking for only one person, usually the individual who was held responsible for a previous killing. It is not considered permissible to kill just anybody who is related to the enemy, for vengeance is directed only against those persons who were directly involved in the original offense.

If the killer and his victim come from very distant communities it is difficult to sustain a simple feud because in order to take revenge the kinsmen of the victim and their allies must travel through several intermediate communities, increasing the risk considerably. In these instances they will attempt to forge alliances with other minimal alliance groups intermediate between them and their enemies which are large enough to allow penetration of the enemies' territory. These alliances result in a *ramified feud*, a state of antagonism between two medial alliance groups, each supplemented by their respective allies who in turn have their own trouble cases to pursue. Thus, a medial alliance not only increases the number of persons involved, but also increases the geographic range in which all can operate, enabling individuals to redress trouble cases which originated in very distant communities. The prevalent mode of combat between two medial alliances in a ramified feud is a large battle, whereas in a simple feud combat is often in the form of short skirmishes and ambushes.

The Tausug system of military and political alliances may profitably be described as "feudal," providing we are careful to define what we mean by that term. In the first place, personal loyalty between leaders and followers is much more important than loyalty to the idea of the group as such. Second, the authority of the leader is restricted by the likelihood that his followers will voluntarily remain loyal; there are few sanctions against recalcitrant followers. Third, leaders on one level of the political system will be followers on another level. Finally, a leader expects loyalty only from those immediately beneath him and in turn gives loyalty only to those immediately above him. It is impossible for a higher leader to command those far beneath him without going through all the intermediate links. In essence, personal loyalty is the keystone of the military and political system of Tausug; loyalty to the leader as such and not to the institution or office which he represents.

## Weapons and Amulets

All Tausug men have a fascination with guns which is comparable to our own concern with automobiles; they love to talk about them, compare them, and shoot them whenever possible. Perhaps 50 percent of all ammunition is used for ceremonial occasions: weddings, births, and similar affairs are usually marked by gunfire. During an eclipse of the moon thousands of rounds were shot, presumably in an effort to recover the moon, although I never pursued the logic of it far enough to fully understand.

*Playing a coin-toss game at a local market. Gambling is a proper pastime for men.*

Most firearms are of World War II vintage obtained by smuggling from the northern parts of the Philippines. Increasing numbers of American rifles from Vietnam are also seen. While repeating and automatic rifles are quite recent, the Tausug have possessed firearms since at least the sixteenth century. In particular, brass cannons were in widespread use against the Spanish, and most pirate ships were equipped with one or more. In addition the Tausug make use of bladed weapons, including the wavy Malay sword or *kris*, and spears— although these are much less important now. Explosive devices are sometimes manufactured from dynamite, and handgrenades are occasionally stolen from the Philippine Constabulary.

Ammunition is smuggled into Jolo or purchased illegally from Philippine authorities. Nevertheless, it is expensive and sometimes in short supply, and is seldom used for target practice. As a result, Tausug are extremely bad marksmen, occasionally filing off the sights from their guns as useless. Emphasis is not on marksmanship, but on gross firepower and mobility. They fight at very close range, often less than 50 yards, and under these conditions automatic weapons are preferred.

Traditional Tausug clothing—very tight pants and shirts for men—has largely disappeared. Battle dress is not particularly distinctive today, nor was special dress for warfare common in the nineteenth century. A young man today will likely be dressed in Western style pants and shirt (often a dark color to avoid detection), ammunition belt or sling, bladed weapon, rifle, amulets, and sometimes a pistol. Most men go without shoes, although imported tennis shoes are common. Tausug men invariably wrap a cloth around their heads—traditionally a turban is considered the mark of a Moslem—which is often inscribed with quasi-Arabic writing to provide a magical effect and protect the wearer from bullets.

Armed combat includes a variety of magical practices, amulets, and divination which are felt to be absolutely essential to sustain a man in battle. However, magic does not interfere with a rational approach to fighting; rather, it is used in situations which are unpredictable by others means. Thus, a Tausug will not trust his fortunetelling books when they tell him to do something which is contrary to common sense. Similarly, an amulet will be discarded if it does not work. The typical Tausug attitude toward amulets was expressed by one

*Although they are primarily symbolic today, most men carry a bladed weapon in addition to their gun; this is an ivory handled kris.*

*Young men wearing amulets as protection against bullets.*

young man: "We do not really trust these amulets because they are just based on guessing; we should really trust God as he is the source of their power. So we just try to find the best one possible." An old priest once refused to guarantee an amulet he had just made for a customer, saying simply, "I am not God."

Amulets, or *habay*, are unusual and rare stones, petrified wood, sea shells, and other items which are tied around the waist, as well as written Arabic spells tied in cloth and worn around the neck or biceps. Their purpose is to prevent the penetration of the body for foreign metal such as knives or bullets. (Understandably, men always insisted on removing their amulets before allowing me to give them a hypodermic injection, for presumably the needle would destroy the amulet's power.) Their faith in the ability of amulets to repel bullets is immense, and a man who is firmly convinced of the worth of his amulets may become reckless in battle. After every battle which I witnessed there were always stories told about men hit by bullets which did not penetrate.

While these stories are partially just optimistic bragging, it is true that the high humidity of the tropical rain forest quickly diminishes the firepower of fresh ammunition; I once pulled a .45 caliber cartridge out of a man's cheek which had not penetrated the bone. Some men also are said to burn their clothes with cigarettes in order to convince their fellows that they are endowed with magical powers to repel bullets. If a man dies in spite of his amulet, it is simply said that the amulets did not work, or that it was his fate to die on that day. If it is the will of God that a man should die, then amulets (whose power is based on that of God) are of no use. There are even some people who deny that amulets are of any use whatsoever; they see a logical contradiction between the belief in amulets and the belief in fate.

In addition to amulets, most men also make use of various techniques of divination in order to insure success in fighting. Various natural signs are taken as auspicious or inauspicious—the appearance of the owl, for example, usually is interpreted as indicating potential trouble—and leaders usually consult fortune telling books before departing for a fight. There are also various spells which are said to increase a man's bravery and capacity to take reckless risks in battle.

## Tactics

In smaller feuds which do not involve a large number of men, as well as instances in which the killer wishes to keep his identity secret, an ambush is usually set up for the intended victim. The most common method is a nighttime foray into the community of the victim, where the group will surprise him as he climbs down from his house in the morning. Another method is to set up an ambush along a path where the enemy is known to travel; this requires knowledge of his habits and is well adapted to the Tausug situation where enemies are well known to each other. In cases where a publicly recognized bond of hostility exists between two men, the ambusher has little motive to keep his identity secret. In other cases where a man has a secret grudge against another, he may attempt to surprise his victim by sneaking under his house at night and shooting through the floor boards. It is for this reason that houses are often fenced, especially if there is reason to anticipate a raid. A killer would normally have a desire to keep his identity secret if the killing were likely to be widely condemned as illegitimate, or if he could not count on much support from kinsmen or friends.

Larger raids or battles involving groups of men often begin with an ambush of another individual or group by moving in force from one community to another. The initial ambush may often be followed by a larger battle after the sound of gunshot brings an assembly of allies to their respective sides. When an attack is anticipated, a leader will usually send for allies to assist him in guarding the community. Not all arrive at the same time. Some come for a day or two and then leave, promising to return if they hear gunfire. Battles are seldom fought by prior arrangement; the offense usually choose a time and place based on practical considerations as well as divination.

There is very little long-range planning in Tausug armed combat; leaders look only to the next anticipated raid or battle. From the point of view of each participant the goals of violence are very short-range and easily obtainable: the death of the specific enemy, vengeance for a stolen animal, and so forth. There is no attempt to drive people out of their homes or obtain control over territory except in very serious cases of land conflict. The construction of tactics is completely pragmatic with a minimum of warfare ritual: there are no ritual combats between leaders, prearranged battles, formal challenges, hero combat, ordeals or any of the other qualities which give much nonliterate warfare its distinctive gamelike quality.

Battles between medial alliance groups are usually fought in forests which afford ample cover and opportunity for mobility. Each minimal alliance group operates as a unit, so once a battle begins there may be very little communication between leaders. Since mobility is extremely rapid and vision is often obscured by the forest, groups sometimes find themselves in a position where they are accidentally firing on men of their own side. The leader goes first and directs his men to various positions.

There is very little precise aiming; guns are often fired rapidly from the waist while running. The most effective fighters use a hit-and-run technique: a forward run in a zig-zag pattern, seeking cover constantly and attempting to move in to the enemy as closely as possible, followed by a temporary retreat to reload. These battle techniques are quite in line with the overall style of Tausug culture: a maximum of opportunity for individualistic personal expression and a minimum of organized group cooperation. There is a complete absence of military discipline in the Western sense; individual decisions and personal bravado predominate.

Enemies sometimes shout insults at each other, such as "You had intercourse with your grandmother," or "Your father fucked a water buffalo." These insults are designed to provoke the enemy to act irrationally out of extreme anger. Their effectiveness stems from the fact that a man is usually fighting against persons whom he knows: former friends, neighbors, or even distant kinsmen, but seldom total strangers. To be insulted by a person with whom one has had previous social relations is always more insulting than to be insulted by a total stranger.

Most men will fight to the death if cornered. While there is some provision for surrender, the rules are very vague and the feasibility of a surrender will depend on the sentiments between the particular men involved. A man would never surrender to a personal enemy, as he probably would be killed anyway. A battle usually does not last more than an hour at most, although assorted skirmishes may continue throughout the day. A group will retreat when their position becomes untenable, when they have exhausted their ammunition, or when they have lost a man, although in very large battles several men may be killed before any decision is reached to retreat. The largest battle in eastern Jolo since World War II (excluding fights with the Philippine army) involved at least 400 men on both sides and a loss of 8 dead.

One very important feature of Tausug combat must be stressed: a large battle between two medial alliance groups is always a very unique configuration of antagonists, it will never again occur in precisely the same form. Tausug warfare is characterized by only a temporary and very vague sense of a "we" or ingroup as opposed to a "they" or outgroup. There is a very strong tendency to locate responsibility for killings in battle in specific persons rather than in the opposing group as a whole; an effort is always made to discover precisely who killed whom. The group which killed one's brother in battle might have only been a temporary aggregate of allies, and it is quite impractical to seek revenge against a group which no longer exists.

Furthermore, the antagonism which a man feels toward members of the other side is intensely personal and directed less against the group as a whole than against specific individuals in a graded series of variable hostility. Thus, a man may strongly wish to kill a particular person on the other side, have a moderate desire to kill a second person, be indifferent to a third, and have a positive desire not to kill a fourth. He may even be unsure that members of his own alliance may not secretly wish to kill him and perhaps use the battle situation as a pretext to shoot him in the back. A man must know much more than merely "we" are fighting "them"; he must know the exact nature of all the ties which bind men to each other in multifarious ways. During one battle Adda was about to shoot at Jul, a man who was at that time supporting his enemies. As he raised his gun, Iburahim, Jul's first cousin (who was then supporting Adda) shouted, "Do not shoot—it's Jul." Adda later told me that it was probable that if he had fired, Iburahim would have shot him in the back for shooting his first cousin.

On another occasion Karrun, a young man who had just recently married a girl whose kinsman had been killed by Rasad, was publicly insulted by some of the allies of his in-laws. Karrun, who had no primary antagonism to Rasad himself, abandoned his wife's kinsmen and formed an alliance with Rasad to seek vengeance for the insult. Neither his wife nor her kinsmen criticized Karrun for doing this, saying "A man's own shame is more important than that of his kinsmen, and his in-laws will understand this if they are good." In the battle which followed, while Karrun was particularly interested in killing certain of his in-laws' temporary allies who had insulted him, he scrupulously avoided shooting at his own in-laws. Furthermore, while Rasad was interested in killing some of Karrun's in-laws, he also refrained from firing at them out of deference to Karrun. Karrun's consanguine kinsmen, on the other hand, did not involve themselves in the battle, being temporarily allied with the people who had insulted Karrun. Rather than fight on either side they remained neutral, waiting during the battle in a nearby orchard. But if their kinsman Karrun had been killed or injured in the fight, they were ready to abandon their alliance with his enemies and instantly join the fight to avenge his death against their former friends.

Almost all battles illustrate similar complexities, and sometimes the distinction between a battle and a brawl is difficult to make. Occasionally three-sided battles occur as a result of a complicated comedy of events in which two groups are fighting, and a third group has withdrawn to fire at anybody who is not related to them. Since there is little coordination between minimal alliance groups, mistakes frequently occur in which a man kills someone he does not intend to kill. This results in hurt feelings and resentments which may blossom into new feuds; the next battle will never be exactly the same as the first.

The complexity of relationships between participants in a feud illustrates in miniature a very important feature of Tausug social structure: the presence of overlapping and criss-crossing ties in which the same men may be torn apart and bound together in multiple ways at the same time. In spite of the constant and endemic conflict in Tausug society, the divisions between men never all run in the same direction; hence the unity of the political system as a whole is preserved in an atmosphere of strife. To use the analogy of a folded piece of paper, if the folds all run in the same direction there is more likelihood of the paper tearing permanently. But Tausug society is more like a crumpled piece of paper in which the strength of the sheet itself is preserved in spite of the folds, precisely because they run counter to each other.[3] Thus, while conflict divides men into antagonistic groups, it also forces men to seek alliances with others which they might not otherwise attempt.

Furthermore, in any conflict between two communities, especially if they are adjacent to each other, there will always be people who have relatives on the other side. These people usually remain neutral and may be instrumental in bringing about a settlement of the case. The ties between two feuding communities are never totally severed; there will always be persons who are able to freely travel between them, bringing gossip and information and perhaps arranging for settlement. Women, children, and the elderly are always *de facto* neutrals; it is considered very shameful to kill them, although sometimes they are hit by accident. Women are sometimes even sent to gather information about the enemy, usually on a ruse of visiting distant kin.

There are a variety of ethical ideas which also serve to limit the ferocity of armed combat. The most general norm is that it is wrong to engage in any behavior which is not immediately directed at the enemy himself. Looting of property is condemned as an end in itself, although it sometimes occurs as a means of further drawing out the anger of the enemy; in most cases the return of the looted property is usually specified as part of the eventual settlement of the case. Mutilation of bodies and torture are condemned and rarely occur, as is fighting in mosques and cemeteries and other holy places. Ethical restrictions

---

[3] Students who are interested in a general discussion of this phenomenon should consult *The Functions of Social Conflict* by Lewis Coser (New York: Free Press, 1956) and *Custom and Conflict in Africa* by Max Gluckman (Oxford: Basil Blackwell, 1956).

are not lessened in fighting non-Tausug; the ethical universalism of Islam (which is similar to Christianity in this respect) is well understood and non-Tausug are not regarded as any the less human. While government soldiers are sometimes hacked and mutilated, this is merely an attempt to reduce morale, not because of their lessened value as human beings. However, violence in Tausug society does have a tendency to go beyond what is considered right by their own standards. Tausug live in a world of violence and believe in violence. But ideally if that violence is to hold value, it must not exceed necessity. The theme of Tausug epic poetry is not violence itself, but an image of man which expresses itself most clearly in violence. Nevertheless, abuse of military and political power is common—and one's fellows will not suffer an abusive person for long. Tausug typically believe that power corrupts and that the moral man and the politically powerful man is a very rare combination; only the sultan can really be both.

## Risk Taking and Piracy

The average Tausug man is not a very cautious sort. It is almost as if he deliberately seeks risky situations, taking chances with a dangerous world. Risk taking in Tausug culture is encouraged, and the prudent lose the opportunity to demonstrate to their fellows valued virtues of character: bravado, honor, masculinity, and even magnanimity. Outlaws, criminals, well-known thieves and the ever-present seekers after revenge are admired as persons of strong character who have demonstrated their willingness to seek dangerous situations, or to accept them voluntarily when luck has made them inevitable. Long epic songs glorify heroes who have excelled in these virtues. An individual may have a fateful situation thrust upon him when he "finds" a case which demands his action, or he may voluntarily seek it through an adventurous piracy mission or by becoming involved in a trouble case when he has no definite moral obligation to do so.

Yet there is a certain style in Tausug risk taking which is not unlike our own seeking of stress in roller coasters or in sky diving: there is always the confident expectation that the danger is really illusory. Both a strongly developed belief in fate as well as the presence of divination, amulets, and other magical means serves to reduce the sense of real risk. A man believes that he has the knowledge and potential to overcome the risk involved in military activity, or if he does not, then the fate of his own death is predetermined beyond human control and he would die anyway.

While adventurous risk taking for its own sake is a style of conduct in all Tausug armed combat, it is seen most clearly in piracy raids to distant islands. It is here that the individual voluntarily assumes a risk without any clear obligation to do so—indeed the act is usually condemned in terms of a higher religious morality. Raids to distant islands combine four elements of fatefulness: genuine danger and risk, the danger of being captured by the Philippine Constabulary, the fatefulness of a character contest, and the fatefulness of gambling and un-expected rewards. While the desire for loot and pecuniary rewards is also important, it is the desire associated with gambling, not the pecuniary gain of everyday work, as there is always a doubt about the outcome of the mission.

When the English adventurer James Brooke was creating his personal petty kingdom on the north coast of Borneo in the early nineteenth century, his difficulties were complicated by the rampant piracy which then prevailed in the Sulu Sea and adjacent waters. In the nineteenth-century Malay world the distinction between trade, piracy, and warfare was very hazy; Tausug would often begin on a strictly trading voyage and then engage in a bit of piracy if the opportunity presented itself. Ships were sometimes raided at sea, although the major goal of raiding expeditions to the Central Philippines was to capture slaves, both for sale within Jolo and as far south as southern Borneo and Java. Loot was also taken if available; on several occasions the Spanish government in Manila made formal requests to the sultan of Sulu to return vestments and religious articles looted from Philippine churches.

Traditional piracy and slaving expeditions were organized by leaders of minimal and medial alliance groups often in groups of several boats. Acts of piracy against Filipino Christians were sometimes justified on religious grounds as part of the *jihad*, or holy war against non-Moslems, although all of my older informants emphatically deny that the sultan would ever directly organize piracy missions because this would be incompatible with his role as head of the religious hierarchy. It is impossible to determine precisely the influence of Islamic religious ideas on piracy and slave raiding in the nineteenth century as they were interpreted by Tausug at that time. My own guess is that then, as now, piracy was condemned in general religious terms, especially by the elderly, but sustained largely by adventure-seeking young men who could safely feel that they would have ample time to concern themselves with the afterlife in their later years. I once asked the headman of Tubig Nangka about a group of young men who had just returned from a raid to Basilan Island. He was in no mood to discuss the matter, but said that the men would surely be punished in the after-life. But his wife later jokingly volunteered the information that her husband had been a skilled cattle thief when younger and had once participated in a raid to several offshore Samal islands.

With the coming of fast ironclad vessels and steam technology in the middle of the nineteenth century, large-scale piracy was eventually controlled by the Spanish, although sporadic slaving trips to nearby islands, especially Basilan and northern Borneo, continued into the early American period. Slaves who grew up in Jolo were generally well treated and often became quite in fluential within the household—although their status in the society at large remained low—largely because a mistreated slave could always run away to a rival headman or appeal for the protection of the sultan. The attitude toward the slave trader was again one of considerable ambivalence: on the one hand, he was admired as an enterprising and courageous individual who was not afraid to take risks, but on the other hand, he was condemned as a thief who dealt in human traffic.

Slavery was quickly eliminated under American pressure, partially because the Tausug emphasis on achieved friendship and alliance made it possible to integrate former slaves into the larger society in terms of those principles. While slavery has almost completely disappeared, the piracy tradition continues in a modified form. Raids today are conducted primarily for loot rather than slaves, and they are usually only undertaken at relatively short distances: 75 miles to Basilan Island or Tawi-tawi Island, or a very occasional raid of 100 miles to Zamboanga. The traffic in smuggled cigarettes from Borneo has created new opportunities for piracy and cargoes are sometimes hijacked in an atmosphere of Byzantine intrigue. More rarely, interisland passenger vessels are held up. Chinese merchants and wealthy Christians are a favorite target, although raids are sometimes conducted against relatively poor isolated settlements of non-Tausug Moslems; in some cases an entire village may be looted. For the most part these activities are conducted by younger men in search of fortune and adventure who in less adventurous moments are simple farmers or fishermen; fulltime "professional" pirates are rare. In Tubig Nangka about 20 percent of the younger men had been on at least one piracy expedition outside of Jolo Island.

The loot taken today reflects the changing material culture of the Tausug: shoes, watches, transistor radios, or sewing machines, as well as cattle, money, jewelry, weapons, brasswork, and gongs. But the social organization of expeditions is largely the same as it was in the nineteenth century: a leader recruits a group of followers—both kinsmen and friends—to accompany him, and may also attempt to join forces with other groups for a larger expedition.

The danger to the group is quite real. In the year prior to my stay in Tubig Nangka about 10 persons from eastern Jolo were killed in an unsuccessful attempt to raid a town in Basilan, and one man had just returned from several years in a Philippine prison for attempting to steal some cattle on Basilan. The headman of Tubig Nangka during World War II was killed by the Japanese during a piracy raid.

But from the point of view of a Tausug man, the risk taking and possibility of death is largely illusory. He deeply feels that these things cannot happen to him because of both the strength of his personal bravery as well as the power of his amulets and other esoteric knowledge. He is seeking danger with the confident expectation that it is not really dangerous. One informant remarked that sometimes people go on raids not only for the loot, but also to "test their amulets and their magical power" and determine if they really work, always, of course, with the hopeful expectation that they do.

# 4

# The Control of Violence

## The Idea of the Law

LIKE MANY ETHNIC GROUPS in the Philippines the Tausug are as obsessed with litigation as they are with the conflict which makes it necessary. While concern with law, including such informal processes such as mediation of disputes, is a widespread Filipino cultural pattern, the influence of Islam has provided an added impetus to the development of legal institutions among the Tausug. Perhaps more than any other major religion, Islam has stressed the importance of legal rules in man's relations with both God and his fellow men. To be a good Moslem is first of all to adhere to the religious law which was derived from the Koran and the traditions interpreting it and which embraces not only ritual obligations, but also a range of matters which we might today consider "secular"— obligations which are nevertheless held by Moslems to be necessary to establish a working community of the faithful on earth.

This legalistic emphasis in Tausug life is apparent at every turn. All legitimate political authorities are regarded primarily as juridical officials; that is, while headmen also perform a variety of nonlegal functions, their authority to do so is always derived from the fact that they are primarily representatives of "the Law." It is their legal role which is the major factor in the definition of their status.

All legal systems must deal with two major issues: the problem of justice and the problem of order (although the matter will seldom be conceptualized quite that explicitly). Law has to insure that justice will be done, or at least that most people think so most of the time. On the other hand, it must also insure that there is order in society, that people are not faced with the nightmare of a war of all against all in which interpersonal conflicts are only solved through brute force. The perennial problem of law is to reconcile these

86

two needs in a culturally satisfactory manner. Some cultures consistently put more emphasis on one or another. An observer in Tausug society is immediately impressed by the fact that Tausug consistently opt for justice rather than order when it is not possible to achieve both at the same time. While there is no specific Tausug word which accurately renders English *justice* (perhaps *buntul* or "straight" is closest) the sense of rightness in the outcome of a case is nevertheless paramount. This striving for justice is so great that it sometimes seems as if they are willing to bring down the whole world in chaos in order to achieve it.[1]

The emphasis on justice is clearly seen in the absence of any ritualistic or arbitrary methods of solving disputes. It is possible for conflicts to be solved by consulting a horoscope or divining from the liver of a chicken, and many peoples in Southeast Asia have adopted methods of legal decision making of precisely this sort. But such methods are completely absent in Tausug culture; conflicts are solved either by reference to the specifics of a system of religious justice, or by mutual agreement among independent persons fully in control of their own interests. Furthermore, there is no Tausug word for compromise, and as an ideal it seems completely absent. Discussion continues until all the litigants are *sulut*, that is, fully satisfied by the terms of the settlement. Although it may sometimes appear to an external observer that a settlement may be achieved by each party "going half way" (in our view compromise involves justice for neither, but order for both), Tausug do not view it in this manner at all. The achievement of order at the expense of justice, as embodied in an arbitrary compromise or decision of a capricious oracle, is quite foreign to the Tausug mind.

A basic Tausug value is that interpersonal conflicts are best discussed publicly rather than kept secret. Conflict should be brought into the open, although always through the intervention of a go-between who provides a buffer between the two disputing parties. Interpersonal conflicts are a universal human problem, but many cultures solve these problems by pushing them off into the realm of the supernatural, setting up elaborate systems of witchcraft and magic which allow people to displace aggression on substitute objects. One is struck with the relative lack of this sort of thing among the Tausug. Faced with a dispute, a man has no other means to solve it other than by a direct confrontation—either through litigation or through violence—with its source.[2]

Definitions of law are many and varied, but for our purposes we can de-

---

[1] One reason a Tausug can behave irresponsibly when angered by an injustice is precisely because he knows he is surrounded by others who will attempt to control his anger. Public expression of anger in modern mass society is disruptive primarily because these informal controls are largely absent.

[2] While there is a belief in witchcraft—the idea that there are evil powers in the world which can be captured by men for malevolent ends—, it is not important; people do not worry about witches and rarely accuse each other of witchcraft. Symbolic aggression toward an enemy (such as a magical curse from a distance) is never regarded as a substitute for actual violence.

fine it as *the institutionalization of ethics in terms of power.* That is, a legal system must minimally possess: 1) a set of ethical norms which specify what is permissible and not permissible; 2) a set of institutions to insure that violations of these norms will be corrected—a system of redress; and 3) some type of organized power, often involving the threat of violence, to insure compliance and put "teeth" into the law. The Tausug term for law is *sara,* derived from the Arabic *shari'a.* As in English the word implies not only the substantive law itself as a collection of rules and norms, but also the authorities, processes, and powers necessary for applying and enforcing the law. A headman not only possesses the law in the sense that he has knowledge of the code, but he is also often described in the third person as "the Law." In formal legal proceedings the headman is not called by his name, but rather is referred to simply as *sara* in deference to the position. The word is used to collectively describe all headmen in Jolo, from the weakest headman up to the sultan himself who is regarded as the highest legal authority.

With reference to the rules themselves, however, the word *sara* can be translated as "rules prescribing justiciable external conduct." That is, the rules are obligatory, binding, and sufficiently precise to serve as the basis for a decision that they have been violated. They must also refer to external conduct: what men do rather than what they merely believe. Within this larger definition, the Tausug recognize several subtypes of law depending upon the source.

First, there is *sara kuraan* (Koranic law) which has as its ultimate source the revelations of God to Mohammed and embodied in the Koran. It refers both to ultimate moral norms as well as to rules for the specific conduct of religious rituals: the proper way to pray, the pilgrimage to Mecca, the giving of tithes, and many others. It is known primarily through holy books, and according to the Tausug is unchanging and eternal. Violations of Koranic law are usually not subject to punishment on earth by man; they are primarily sins against God who will Himself assume the task of punishing the offender in the afterworld.

Second, there is interpreted religious law, or *sara agama,* which consists of a body of rules created primarily—although not exclusively—by the sultan in a religious context. Most Tausug legal officials maintain that the difference between *sara kuraan* and *sara agama* is necessary since the rigid rules of pure Koranic law are impractical in some criminal and civil matters because of their severity, thereby requiring more usable interpretation. Thus, the chopping off of the hand of a thief is often given as an example of pure Koranic law, but it is widely admitted that nobody but a total fool would allow his hand to be cut off, and such penalties were rarely if ever enforced. Sometimes religious leaders will exhort people in a legal discussion with the strict enforcement of Koranic law ("If we were really enforcing the law, we would chop off his hand"), but this is done primarily to set the tone for the discussions in proper religious perspective, as well as to assure others that they are really "men of law."

Much *sara agama* is codified in a written lawbook issued by the sultan. These codes, or *diwan,* were issued anew by each sultan after consultation with religious advisors, influential royalty, and various headmen. The oldest code which has been preserved dates from the 1860s, and new codes were issued by successive sultans. The earliest codes prescribed fines in terms of various trade goods, but recent codes all give fines in Philippine currency. Typical offenses for which punishments and fines are listed include adultery, fornication, abduction of women, elopement, sodomy, slander, telling lies to make people fight, theft, bestiality, and murder of close kinsmen, among others. For murder of non-kinsmen, suggested amounts of blood money are fixed, and payments for a wounding are prescribed according to the severity of the wound. Some aspects of marriage and family law are also codified.

It must not be thought that the Tausug *diwan* is comparable in any but a superficial way to modern statutory law. In the first place, the codes are used not to legislate social change or even the whims of the sultan, but rather to standardize existing customs and religious ideas. In the second place, there is always local variation in the enforcement and applications of the rules, although ideally they are uniform. Finally, certain offenses are conspicuously absent from the *diwan*: land law, inheritance law, commercial law, some offences against honor, and others. A rule is typically included in the code only when there is some need for standardization, such as the payment of bridewealth in abductions, or when the offense is regarded both as a sin against God and a crime against man equally, especially—an offense against God (such as incest) which is likely to rebound against the whole community.

Finally, there is customary law, or *sara adat*, the uncodified traditions and customs of the community which have legal significance. Not all customs have such significance; an offense must be sufficiently serious and likely to cause interpersonal conflict and possible violence to be considered justiciable. Murder, assault, theft, and many offenses involving honor are usually considered questions of *sara adat*, although they have religious dimensions as well. Payment of debts, inheritance, and land tenure are also included. Customary law is regarded as purely man-made, without a revealed religious origin and subject to considerable change and interpretation depending on the circumstances, as opposed to *sara agama* which has a sacred origin and is more fixed and immutable. Customary law is most closely associated with the community headman, while *sara agama* is ultimately the province of the sultan.

The various types of law are not regarded by the Tausug as really contradictory. It is only necessary that the lower forms should be consistent with the spirit, though not necessarily the letter, of the higher forms. Thus there is much room for modification in actual practice, as in the following statement by one religious leader:

> In warfare it may be that a man is wounded by having a spear thrust into him. The headman may attempt to settle the case by suggesting that blood money be paid for the wound. In the real law based solely on the Koran the man should also have a spear thrust into him to make things even, but that would just create

more trouble. So the headman applies customary law to achieve settlement. But if the headman is sincere, the customary law goes along with the spirit of the religious law.

The ultimate goal of all forms of law is the achievement of *karayawan*, a word which means goodness, peace, ritual purity, tranquility, happiness, or pleasure, depending on the context in which it is used. The correct adherence to the ritual obligations and ethical imperatives of Islam as embodied in the *sara kuraan* produces *karayawan* in the afterlife: the pleasures and rewards of heaven. Adherence to religious law embodied in *sara agama* results not only in *karayawan* for the individual in the afterlife, but also in the ritual purity of the community and the absence of God's curse against the community of man. Finally, the proper mediation of disputes within the realm of *sara adat* brings peace, goodness, and tranquility to the participants in the dispute as well as to the entire community. *Karayawan*, thus, is the ultimate embodiment of the morally good as achieved through adherence to the law in all its forms.

By the standards of modern statutory law, with its emphasis on internal consistency and a specialized legal logic, Tausug law seems quite vague. With the exception of a few rules which are quite explicit—involving precise fines and punishments for certain religious crimes—and embodied in the *diwan*, the idea of the law serves primarily to provide a traditional ideology for the settlement of disputes without finding therein a clear basis for the decision of concrete cases. Thus, the most generalized goal of the sacred law is said to be that settlement of disputes is better than fighting between men. For example, it would be said that two cousins fighting over the ownership of a motor boat should settle their trouble amicably, but this "judgment" typically takes no account of the actual specifics needed to bring about such a settlement, which will always have to be unique to the particular case. The basic characteristic of Tausug law is the presence of a general statement of a moral precept derived from either religious law or traditional customs coupled with a concrete application to the case in terms of more immediate ethical and practical considerations: "It is written, but I say unto you. . . ." Tausug are not bothered by the lack of consistency in the application of the law to particular cases, while always maintaining that the law itself—being ultimately religiously inspired—nevertheless comprises a unitary whole derived from the expression of God's will.

## The Community and Headman

In spite of widespread conflict, Tausug regard their society as a whole inasmuch as it reflects the idea of a unitary law (*sara*) mirrored in the sultanate and its institutions, a unitary religion (*agama*), and a unique style of life and set of customs (*adat*). The idea of the sultanate as a locus for the self-image of Tausug society has been partially replaced by the idea of incorporation into the modern Philippine nation-state, but religion, law, and custom are still the major points of reference in terms of which the average Tausug defines his society and his place within it.

The concept of the law is of primary importance. Ideally the law is universal, and cases can be adjudicated by any legitimate legal official within the realm without regard to his location, although in practice persons tend to go to the headman in their own community or region. In cases of abduction and elopement of women, however, the couple will often escape to a distant headman to have the union legitimized; since the law is universal, it follows that it can be applied by any person authorized to do so.

Persons who have the authority to act as *sara* include all local and regional headmen who have been given titles by the sultan to symbolize this role, all religious officials, and all aristocrats who hold the title of *datu*. Typically, religious leaders accompany headmen to legal discussions. But unless the religious leader possesses political power and influence in his own right, his function at the case seems to be limited to giving vague oratory invoking the Koran, the will of God, and so forth. Some cases— primarily marital disputes—may be settled directly by religious leaders with the headman's approval, and these cases are sometimes held within the mosque to give an aura of religious sanctity to the proceedings. But in the settlement of cases involving homicide, the role of the priest is distinctly subsidiary to the role of the headman. Some people cynically told me that priests had nothing to do at legal discussions except "talk about nothing, chew betel, and spit." Some religious leaders, however, have considerable political power, but this must be distinguished from their religious role.

Similarly, all those who hold the title of *datu* are entitled to act as "the Law." Datus represent an estate of aristocrats who have inherited their title patrilineally[3]; they comprise about 2 percent of the adult population, although there are more datus in those regions which were the sites of the traditional sultanate. In Tausug theory all datus are related patrilineally to one of the previous sultans of Sulu (back to at least the fifteenth century), although very few will be able to trace the exact relationship. Many datus act as headmen in the areas where they live. In practice, however, datus who lack the power and wealth necessary to sustain the title will tend to drop it, since the use of a title which is not backed by actual social reality is regarded as shameful to the individual and humorous to others. This illustrates an important feature of the use of titles within the Tausug political system: the title does not in itself confer power, but merely symbolizes and gives legitimacy to power which the leader has already acquired.

In addition to legal functions, which will be discussed later, a headman also engages in a number of other activities. Within the mosque he often sits at the front during prayer and makes decisions which do not require specialized religious knowledge, such as deciding who will lead the ritual that day. Along with

---

[3] Inheritance of property or succession to a title in the *patrilineal* line means inheritance from the father or father's kinsmen. A woman may inherit from her father, but she does not pass the property down to her children.

religious leaders, he mobilizes resources for the upkeep of the mosque. He is a key person in the appointment and promotion of religious officials. He can organize people for cooperative labor, such as cleaning the community cemetery, or repairing a waterhole (although community-wide activities of this sort are not common). He may own a small market or cockfighting ring and receive revenue from market and gambling fees, and he is obliged to settle cases and keep the peace. One of his major functions is to represent the community in dealings with other headmen and more recently with Philippine government officials. When people visit the community for any reason (visiting headmen, health officials, Army officers, politicians seeking election, government judges, and others), the primary burden of entertaining them falls upon the local headman. Tausug are quite proud of their traditional hospitality—it is considered very rude not to offer food to a visitor—, and the headman may request chickens and other food from his followers to feed a visiting notable and his party.

A key feature of Tausug culture is underscored if we contrast the typical conduct of a headman and legal official with the protagonists in a feud. Persons who are pursuing feuds to enhance their material interests or to sustain their personal honor invariably act in terms of an "ethics of ultimate commitment"[4] in which there is an uncompromising singleness of purpose inspired by their sense of duty to some absolute value without regard for the long-range consequences. As a result of such an orientation, means have a tendency to justify ends, and the eventual consequences of the act are seldom taken into account. In an intellectual sense a Tausug understands that one killing will invariably lead to another killing—that self-help in the long run is self-defeating—but such considerations do not normally affect his conduct if he feels obligated to vindicate his shame and honor in the public view. He is oriented with an implicit ethic of "a man does rightly and leaves the outcome to God."

The headman, on the other hand, is motivated by an "ethics of responsibility" which recognizes that it is not always possible to achieve perfect good in this world. He knows that violence and feud often have unforeseen consequences, both for the persons involved as well as the wider community, which take precedence over the more immediate demands of shame and honor. In order to achieve a possible solution, he must sometimes disregard his own ethical commitments and substitute instead a higher sense of responsibility in which order and peace are more important than perfect justice. In exercising their power in this way, headmen often must engage in acts which are condemned from a purer, more uncompromising sense of ethics. The headman of Tubig Nangka killed a number of men in his lifetime, some as a direct consequence of his role as headman; yet, he often wondered whether God would not punish him for murder—there is a saying that headmen often go to hell. The paradox of Tausug

---

[4] The phrase is Max Weber's; see his "Politics as a Vocation" in *From Max Weber* (Ed. H. H. Gerth and C. W. Mills, Oxford University Press, 1946).

headmanship (and probably the universal problem of politics) is that while the headman is ideally a representative of a pure religious law, the achievement of that law requires behavior which is itself condemned.

The most important characteristic of the headman's relationship to the community is the fact that power is ultimately over people and not over territory. A Tausug leader is always a leader of men, and only through them does he have any claim on the territory in which they live.[5] A headman acquires followers through his personal charisma and leadership ability, the use of his ties of kinship, and the manipulation of alliances based on friendship. Since territory is not itself the basis of political groups in Tausug society, the territorial base of each headman will vary with the extent of his own personal influence. Some headmen control a much wider territory than others and may even have pockets of followers in the territory nominally associated with another headman, and headmen from different parts of the island sometimes swear friendship with each other.

The primary locus of the power of a headman will begin at his own house and his own close kinsmen who immediately surround it. Moving out from this center, his power will typically decrease until it begins to overlap the territory of another headman. Persons who live on the fringes may give nominal loyalty to both headmen, although many exceptions could be noted in given instances. In practical everyday terms, one can obtain a rough indication of the power of a headman in rural Jolo by considering a number of criteria: How many followers does he have? How much wealth does he command? Does he have any titles which symbolize power? How many guns does he command? Is his power based on wisdom and good judgment, or is it based on force alone? The most important criterion, however, is the number of people he can summon, from how far, and for what purposes, and the number of people who regularly bring cases to him to settle.

We may describe the headman's own community as a zone of primary authority: an area from which cases will come to him for settlement, and in which he has direct power to initiate cases against person accused of committing grave moral sins calling for community sanction. Second, there is a zone of secondary authority (in Tubig Nangka this embraced two adjacent communities which shared a common mosque with Tubig Nangka) in which the headman may handle cases which could not be settled locally; he is a first-level appellate judge. Finally, there is a zone of influence from which people may bring cases for settlement if they wish, but where the headman has few rights to initiate

---

[5] Contrast this view with modern Western society in which membership in many political groups is assigned solely on the basis of residence (or residence at birth): membership in the nation, state, county, etc. Such a view is totally different from Tausug ideas. Even during government elections rural Tausug find it very difficult to understand the idea of voting strictly in the district of residence; people often vote where their major alliances are, even if this means crossing the imaginary lines set up by the national government.

cases himself or summon people without their permission. These three zones also correspond to a similarly decreasing power to engage in acts which are not directly related to the legal system, such as organizing mosques, appointing religious officials, collecting market fees, and others.

Spatially the Tausug political system might be described as a series of concentric circles of decreasing power radiating from various points and blending with each other at the edges. Some headmen are more powerful than others; their "circles" are naturally larger. Even the sultan himself—who is really a kind of overall headman—has more power in the region around the capital than he does among his more remote subjects. In the nineteenth century certain leaders would often acquire regional prominence and widespread influence in an area perhaps embracing as many as 10 to 15 communities, although there were always minor headmen in the same areas as well. Today the locus of regional prominence has largely shifted to partially Westernized Tausug who operate within the framework of Philippine electoral politics.

Headmen are integrated into the Tausug state in terms of their possession of a title given to them by the sultan which symbolizes their power and status, and gives them the right to act as "the Law." Titles are always given on the basis of a community consensus, as well as the sultan's assessment of the actual power

*Headman (center) discussing a feud.*

and status of the prospective headman. In Tausug theory the ideal qualities of a headman are seven: He must be brave and courageous; most headmen were military leaders when they were younger. He must be intelligent and quick-witted. He must be sympathetic and fair. He must be skilled in the use of rhetoric and know how to speak persuasively and logically. He must be knowledgeable in law and religion. He must be willing to travel and render service by settling cases. Finally, he must possess esoteric knowledge and magic (*ilmu*).

In addition to the above, it is obvious that a headman must also possess power and the respect of his followers. The power of a headman is largely a reflection of the number of followers he has: persons who will regularly support him both militarily and economically. Most headmen have a core group of younger men—usually kinsmen living in his home community—who can be counted upon to provide support when it becomes necessary to enforce a decision through force. In Tubig Nangka this group consisted of about 25 armed men whose support was virtually guaranteed, as well as a larger group of followers who might provide help in certain circumstances. In addition, he must have the respect of all those persons in the region who bring cases to him to settle; a headman who acquires a reputation for being overly arbitrary or self-seeking will not remain influential for long. The headman of Tubig Nangka had acquired part of his influence by attracting followers away from a regionally influential headman in a nearby community who had alienated many people by gambling away a considerable sum of money he had collected to repair the mosque, as well as by other outrageous acts. But he was not formally deposed (there is no official procedure to "remove" a headman); rather, his followers gradually stopped bringing cases to him and taking his advice, and soon he was left with little more than his title. Thus, the authority of a Tausug headman depends on the probability that his followers will choose to remain faithful.

Wealth and command over resources is another source of a headman's power. In particular, extensive ownership of land enables him to acquire the political support of those to whom he may lend the land. Headmen are always wealthier than the average persons through the ownership of land, working animals, boats, coconut farms, and firearms. They can often be identified by their outward demeanor and general bearing: they wear better clothing and jewelry, own an above-average-quality bladed weapon or gun, and are often surrounded by a number of younger bodyguards.

There is also an element of inheritance in the acquisition of a title, and the son of a headman sometimes inherits his father's position (although succession is never automatic and must always be authorized by the sultan). In the past headmen sometimes kept genealogies to validate their staus; ideally succession was in the patrilineal line, although there may be a few female links in the genealogy as well. But for the most part the office of headman is an achieved position in which ancestors count very little; talent and ability are much more important. Occasionally women may act as legal officials, although they cannot receive titles. Sometimes a headman's wife will informally take over his role when he dies. The wife of the headman of Tubig Nangka had considerable influence in her own right and often assisted her husband in settling cases which came to him.

A person who possesses wealth, power, and the other essential qualities of a headman, as well as the support of his community and the good graces of the sultan, will eventually be given a title to formally mark his status. The headman of Tubig Nangka says that people began to bring cases to him to settle about two years before he actually received his title of *panglima*; when it was apparent to everyone that he was a headman in a *de facto* sense, it was decided to make this fact official. The proclamation (*paggulal*) of headmanship is usually made by the sultan in a very simple ceremony. (With the exception of the sultan himself there is little ritual which surrounds political office—it is the reality of power which really counts.)

In Tausug theory there is a hierarchy of ranked political offices ranging from the informal community headman (*tau maas*, literally "old man") which does not require official appointment, through a series of appointed offices represented by the titles *laksamana, ulangkaya, majaraja, panglima*, and others.[6] Headmen are ranked by the level of the title they possess; however, the ranking is not viewed as a formal chain of command, but rather as a qualitative reflection of power and status.

Thus, the *panglima* is technically higher than the *majaraja*, but this does not necessarily mean that the higher office can issue commands to the lower office. It means only that at the time the title was first given it reflected a certain level of the headman's actual power and influence relative to other titleholders. However, two titles of the same rank will never be put next to each other (in order "to avoid jealousy"), and the title is given for life (there is little sense of being able to "move up" through promotion). A person will normally keep his title even though he may have lost the power which originally sustained it; as a result, the title system in any given region will seldom accurately reflect the actual balance of power.

The significance of the title system is therefore primarily symbolic, although its importance in this context should not be underestimated. The fact that all titles are ideally related to all others in a larger system, the fact that the title is originally given only by the sultan, and the fact that it legitimizes the right of the holder to act as the Law gives to the individual officeholder a sense of belonging to a larger whole and does serve to temper his tendency to act solely in his own self-interest. For example, the *de facto* headman in Tubig Nangka during World War II was a notorious murderer who was said to operate solely through fear. Some of his followers once suggested that he be given a title, and the sultan approved, probably because a titled headman is easier to control. But he refused

---

[6] Many features of the traditional state organization—including the words for the various titles—are borrowings from Malay. Malay was much more widely spoken as a second language for trade in the past than it is today.

to accept the title for precisely that reason: to become the Law would be to accept a grave responsibility which would interfere with his other nefarious activities.

The notion of a hierarchy of legal officials, however vague in operation, also serves to relate headmen to each other through a system of sharing fines and legal fees. This source of revenue—which can be quite considerable—should ideally be shared with the sultan and other intermediate legal officials. The exact amount to be given to the sultan varies considerably, but ideally it is usually said to be 50 percent. However, there is no system of record keeping, and the sultan is seldom in a position to force payment from recalcitrant headmen; payment depends largely on the goodwill of individual headmen. In the nineteenth century there was probably more strictness about this system of sharing fines, but undoubtedly headmen in remote regions could often defy the sultan. Today headmen who still maintain a sense of obligation to the sultan usually give him his share, along with other gifts, during Maulud-al-nabi, the annual celebration of the birth of the Prophet Mohammed. This ceremony is given in every community during the month of Mohammed's birth, but the opening ceremony is always performed first in the sultan's home mosque. It is attended by loyal headmen from throughout the Sulu Archipelago. There were about 40 headmen present at the occasion in 1967, although in the past considerably more attended. It serves as a major symbolic affirmation of the unity of the Tausug state: a mass offering of tribute and homage.

The title system also operates as a means for regulating appeals. If one of the parties to a dispute is dissatisfied with a decision, he may take the case to a headman with a higher title, for example, from *majaraja* to *panglima*. However, if the *panglima* has less actual power (which may be the case if he has lost influence since first receiving his title), the appeal might go directly to the sultan. While most cases are settled locally, it is possible to initiate cases with the sultan himself, although this happens primarily when two headmen are feuding. In cases which are appealed to a higher authority, the lower headman is usually summoned as a witness to the original case.

## Judgment, Arbitration, and Mediation

Having described the Tausug idea of the law and the social organization of legal authority, we can now look more closely at the actual processes of adjudication. Three basic kinds of procedure are recognized: judgment (*paghukum*) by a competent authority, arbitration (*paghukum muslihat*), and mediation (*pagsalasay*) by a go-between. In judgmental procedures a strict application of the law is made to the case at hand by the headman; the primary concern is the facts of the case, while the feelings of the litigants are irrelevant. In pure mediation, on the other hand, the determination of factual truth is largely irrelevant to the mediator (although obviously important to the litigants)—indeed the facts of the case make the case even more difficult to settle—,while the issues of shame and honor are primary. Arbitration is an intermediate procedure in which both factual right and amicable settlement are equally important. Certain offenses ideally call for judgment, while others call for mediation, but an extremely powerful headman might be able to impose a judgment in a case where a weaker headman might only have been able to mediate, and a weak headman might have to mediate a case which ideally calls for judgment. Nevertheless, headmen are always very clear whether they are judging or mediating with respect to any given case.

The clearest example of *paghukum* (judgment) occurs in cases of religious sins which are also regarded as offenses against the community and general moral order ("vice" in our terminology): sexual offenses (adultery, bestiality, fornication, sodomy, touching an unmarried woman, and others), abduction of women and other marriage affairs, and parricide (killing a close kinsman). Sins such as blasphemy, drunkenness, or flagrant refusal to perform the most elementary religious obligations are also included, but very rarely occur (I never witnessed such cases). Divorce and most family law are also handled primarily through judgment.

The goal of the law in these cases is the punishment of the offender or settlement of the case based on the determined facts. The headman's concern with strict factual truth and strict punishment stems from the fact that many of these religious sins are thought to result in a curse directed at the entire community of the culprit in the form of a prolonged drought. The sinner must be punished and the offense rectified if the well-being of the community is to be restored. But the fact that the community (or "public") in Tausug society is such a vague and nebulous group, with few clear boundaries in either kinship or territory, means that responsibility for action against the criminal falls squarely on the headman who is the only fixed point of reference in the Tausug sense of community. A crime against the community is conceptualized as a crime against the Law: both the law as a body of written rules as well as the person of the headman. In fact, headmen often become extremely angry at offenses of this kind, acting as if the offender had committed a personal affront to his honor.

A typical example of *paghukum* occurred in Tubig Nangka concerning the charge of adultery and incest against Ilu, who was said to have committed sexual relations with her husband's brother. They had been divorced several months before the case occurred, but the accusation implied that the offense had taken place while they were still married. An unsigned note written in Arabic script had been placed on a tree near a small market in a neighboring community and was brought to the headman of Tubig Nangka because there was no strong headman there who could take responsibility for the case. The letter read:

> This letter should be given to the Law. I want to inform him that Rabi and Ilu were behaving like married people when she was still married to his brother Asbarim. Think well about this case, because it is a sin to our place. Do not let them swear that they are innocent, because it is really true that they have done this bad thing.

The headman immediately sent for the woman, although Rabi was away and could not be reached. The ability to summon people is an important feature of a headman's power; if she had refused (which rarely occurs), she would have been brought by force. The case was heard on the headman's front porch; the only other people present were a religious leader, the man who found the note, and some female kinsmen of the woman. There was little legal formality or ritual, although the headman was addressed as "the law," and people did not interrupt each other as they might do in normal conversation.

The woman denied the charge, and a kinsman said that while Ilu and her husband were living with her, she had no knowledge of an affair with his brother. The headman said that if she was really innocent she should swear on the Koran that she did not do it. The *imam* pointed out that if the person who wrote the note could be found and would swear that he had witnessed the crime, then she would be presumed guilty. He also delivered a long lecture on the horrors of a strict Koranic punishment for incest, directing it at Ilu.

Although Ilu wanted to swear immediately, the headman decided that he would wait three days for the person who wrote the letter to make himself known; if he did not, then she would be asked to take the oath. The man who found the letter was asked to announce at the market that any persons having knowledge of the crime should come forward.

Three days later—with no word received from the writer of the letter—Ilu confessed to her sister, who informed the headman. She apparently feared the supernatural punishment for a false oath more than the human punishment for the crime; in addition, punishment in this world would wipe out any further retaliation by God in the afterlife. The headman had surmised she was guilty on the first day because of her nervousness and refusal to look him in the eye; he wisely knew that if he allowed her to take the oath, she probably would have perjured herself out of shame in the face-to-face hearing. It is believed that a curse will rebound on a headman who knowingly allows a person to falsely swear.

The punishment in these cases is standardized according to the *diwan*: payment of a fine of P105 ($25) and a ritual whipping of 105 lashes, followed by a ritual washing of absolution in the ocean. The washing in the ocean is necessary to allow the sin to float away into the sea, a common religious theme in several other contexts as well. The whipping is done very lightly, more symbolic than real. The fine was split between the woman's husband and the headman. Rabi, the other culprit, had left for Tawi-tawi Island; he would be punished if he returned, with the entire fine going to the headman.

*Hukum muslihat* may be described as a type of arbitration in which a judgment is imposed which reflects both the determined facts of the case as well as the desire of litigants for an amicable settlement. The goal of the procedure is to find the truth and then embody it in the form of a settlement which is satisfactory to all. While a judgment will be made by legal officials, there are no fines or punishments. It is used primarily in disputes over the ownership of property, inheritance problems, conflicts about the payment of debts, bridewealth controversies, and some cases of theft where the identity of the thief must be proven.

An example of this procedure occurred when Indang, a woman from a nearby community, came to the headman of Tubig Nangka to request settlement of a dispute between her son and Adjibun, one of the headman's followers. She came to the headman of Tubig Nangka because Adjibun lived there and because there was no strong headman in her own community. A headman will usually accept a case between one of his own followers and a person from another community, unless the two communities are not on good terms with each other for some reason.

Indang's late husband had owed Adjibun fifty pesos. Several months after his death his stepson Latip sold an outrigger boat to a minor headman in an adjacent community for 200 pesos. Adjibun heard about the sale and went to the headman to ask for 50 pesos of the purchase price to satisfy the debt, assuming that he had a share in the boat which had originally belonged to the stepfather. However, Latip denied that Adjibun had a share in the boat, saying that it belonged solely to his mother Indang. The minor headman decided to withhold the money and give it to the headman of Tubig Nangka pending settlement of the dispute.

A hearing was held the next day in his house. Adjibun claimed that after Latip's stepfather died, he went to his house to ask for payment of the debt, and Latip assured him that he would be given a share of the boat. Latip answered that he had made no such commitment as the boat was not his to give. Adjibun implied that Latip was lying and said that he would either swear on the Koran that Latip had promised the share, or accept Latip's oath that he had not said it. The headman pointed out that the property was actually Indang's and that if her son had promised it to Adjibun, he had done so without her permission. Latip agreed, saying that he was not in a position to commit the property. The headman decided that the money for the boat should be given entirely to Indang.

However, there was still the question of whether Latip could be held liable for 50 pesos because of his alleged promise to Adjibun. The headman told the two men to think whether they would be willing to swear concerning the facts of the case and to be present at the mosque the following Friday, bringing any witnesses to the original conversation. In the meantime, however, an unrelated killing had taken place, and the case was not heard as scheduled. Several days later, the headman sent word to Latip that he should come to swear that he had not promised a share to Adjibun. Latip replied that he did not wish to swear and would send the money to Adjibun immediately.

In cases of this type the major means for the determination of the truth lies in the use of witnesses, as well as the threat of curse if an oath is falsely given. However, Tausug have no notion comparable to our idea of the neutral witness; it is assumed that all witnesses are biased in favor of one party, although not necessarily liars. A person having knowledge of events in a case detrimental to a kinsmen or friend would simply refuse to testify or would deny knowledge of the events.

Judgment is sometimes also given in cases which normally could be subject to mediation between the opposing parties, but where there is a very great difference in the level of power between them. A good example of this situation occurred when a Samal was accused of stealing some oysters from the oyster bed of one of the sultan's relatives. Oysters are raised for mother of pearl primarily by persons strong enough to insure the safety of the beds while most of the labor is provided by offshore-dwelling Samals.

Datu Samman suspected that he was losing large oysters and began marking them secretly for recognition. Several months later a man offered to sell him a large oyster shell which had clearly been stolen from his own bed. The shell was traced to a neighboring headman, Maas Laling, who claimed to have bought it from one of Datu Samman's own Samal retainers. The culprit refused to admit his guilt, even with Maas Laling as a witness, and was taken into a shed and beaten until he confessed. Although Datu Samman was a legal official in his own right, it is considered more appropriate to give the case to another headman. Mukarabin, the headman of Tubig Nangka, was visiting at the time, and the case was given to him for judgment.

The case was discussed on the beach under conditions which reflected the lower status of the Samal: he was made to squat on the beach while the others stood over him, and everyone laughed when he publicly admitted to having stolen the oyster (a Tausug will seldom admit to wrongdoing in a face to face encounter; the fact that a Samal will do so is said to indicate their "lack of shame"). The Samal said that Maas Laling knew it was stolen when he bought it and had promised to protect him in case of trouble. While Mukarabin knew that his accusation was probably true, he wished to avoid any further trouble between Laling and Datu Samman, so he told the Samal that a person who is a thief can also be presumed to be a liar and that if Laling and Samman should fight over this issue, he would personally kill him. He fined the luckless Samal 52 pesos and the cost of the stolen oyster. The significance of this case lies in the fact that if both the litigants had been Tausug it would have been handled very differently: there would be mediation instead of judgment (especially if the two were of equal power) and no fine would have been imposed.

The primary offenses dealt with by mediation (*pagsalasay*) are murder, major theft, serious land conflicts, and various offenses involving insults to honor. The outstanding characteristic of legal procedure in mediation is the irrelevance of the facts of the case to the mediator; settlement does not involve "looking for the truth" but rather "looking for goodness" (*karayawan*). The skilled mediator must be an excellent diplomat and shrewd judge of character; he must know how to separate the emotional issues of shame and honor from the actual material interests of the feuding parties in order to bring about an amicable settlement. In order to achieve settlement it is often necessary for the mediator to lie cleverly, denying the existence of negative feelings between those who are fighting, and stressing to each party that the other is really afraid and willing to accept settlement, even if this is not actually true.

During the course of negotiations in a serious feud, the opposing parties are never brought face-to-face: the danger of violence is usually too great. The first task of the headman is to convince the parties to "give him the case," that is, agree to enter into serious discussions eventually leading to some sort of settlement. He will often travel between opposing factions for discussion and sometimes will arrange for a meeting between two older men representing the feuding parties. The principals never attend these initial exploratory meetings themselves; if they did, people might then say that they are overly anxious for settlement—feuding persons try to maintain at least the public appearance of being steadfast in their resolution to accept nothing less than perfect justice.

Once the terms of a settlement are informally agreed upon, the parties may be brought together for a formal confrontation, always under the watchful eye of a number of armed neutrals, including the headman's bodyguards. There is a studied formality at these confrontations where speech is deliberate and purposeful (Tausug say "real speech") and considerable serenity is maintained. Sometimes the feuding parties will be asked to swear on the Koran that they will refrain from further fighting. To deliberately break the terms of a settlement is to risk making an enemy of the headman who arranged it, who will usually join forces with the other side in active hostility to the party who "put the law to shame."

One important difference between *paghukum* and *pagsalasay* procedures is the fact that the legal norms are much more specific in judgment than in mediation. Furthermore, in judgmental procedures the headman gives his decision based merely upon the single issue in question. In mediation, on the other hand, there are often multiple conflicts between the opposing factions, all of which must be settled at the same time if violence is to be avoided. The mediator is less limited by formal law and is forced to take account of the multiple relationships and conflicts which divide the feuding parties—which may be quite complicated.

This is illustrated by the case of the conflict between Dilu and Tuwasil who were fighting over the ownership of some coconut trees, a dispute over some stolen property, a broken sewing machine, a case of possible adultery, and a number of other matters. In addition each man had a number of friends and allies who in turn had their own trouble cases with persons on the other side. One battle had already been fought, and although there were about 30 guns on each side, fortunately nobody had been killed. All of the local headmen, including Mukarabin of Tubig Nangka, were desperately trying to arrange a truce before a death occurred, which would make settlement even more difficult.

A preliminary meeting was held among several of the headmen in the region, including older men who represented many of the feuding alliance groups. It was agreed that the case was so complicated that outside help was needed in order to achieve settlement. Mukarabin went the next day by boat to see the sultan and request his presence, or at least a representative, as the prestige of the sultan would add to the possibility of an amicable settlement. He agreed, and a meeting was arranged for the following day with a kinsman of the sultan who arrived by boat with several bodyguards armed with automatic rifles.

In the meantime the situation had deteriorated to the point where both groups were ready to fight at any moment; it was clear that if a truce was not arranged that day, they would surely fight after the sultan's representative had left. An initial meeting was held at the house of one of the neutrals in the case—a person who had kinsmen on both sides—in which the sultan's representative emphasized the need for settlement and said he would be willing to personally contribute money if it would help.

Dilu had originally seized a coconut harvest of some trees belonging to Tuwasil by driving his sister out of the house near where they were planted. He did this because he had been arrested (later released) by the Philippine Constabulary for a murder which he had not committed, and he suspected Tuwasil of leading the soldiers to his house (it is almost impossible for Philippine government authorities to capture a man without the help of his local enemies). Tuwasil and his sister were sent for; they said they wanted the money from the coconut harvest returned, as well as a sewing machine and a piggy bank stolen from her house. The sultan's representative told them not to worry, adding that he would pay for those items himself if necessary.

Mukarabin then walked half a mile to Dilu's house where he had assembled with about ten of his armed allies. He denied taking the sewing machine and told Mukarabin that even if Tuwasil agreed to pay for the gun which the Constabulary had confiscated he would still fight because of shame. He said, "We were forced to run in the previous battle because of lack of ammunition. Everyone is laughing at us; we will just have to fight them again."

Mukarabin returned to the meeting with the sultan's representative and told him that he could not convince Dilu to accept a settlement. In the meantime Tuwasil said he would accept payment for the coconuts and would not worry further over the fact that his sister had been temporarily driven from her house because he had been able to throw stones at Dilu's house in turn. The sultan's representative said that he would personally go to see Dilu and encourage him to accept the settlement, adding for rhetorical effect that "if they do not respect me I will break their guns over their heads."

They met with Dilu in an open field near his house. Dilu blamed Tuwasil for his humiliation by being captured by the Constabulary and said he took the coconuts to make up for his lost gun. It was apparent that he wanted to fight, and one of his allies asked for two days' time to think about the request for settlement. But Dilu's mother, who was worried about her son, whispered to the headman of Tubig Nangka that they were planning to fight against Tuwasil again that very night. Responding to pressure from the sultan's representative and the headman of Tubig Nangka—who later told me that they would have thrown their own military support against whichever side refused to settle—, Dilu agreed to take an oath of peace with Tuwasil out of "deference to the law." Tuwasil was summoned and the oath was administered by one of the old men; eight persons swore together, including two military leaders from Tubig Nangka (who were included to symbolize the headman's interest in the preservation of the peace) and several other neutrals.

As a sequel to this case, it must be noted that neither Dilu nor Tuwasil were given sufficient time to consult with their numerous allies prior to the swearing. Some of these allies were offended. There is a Tausug saying about this: "When we fight together we first confer, so when we settle we must also confer." The desire of these allies to fight was still strong, and the oath was later broken because some of the participants had greater loyalty to their allies than to their partners in the oath. Dilu later fought against a large alliance group which included Tuwasil, but he told me that during the battle he tried to avoid shooting at Tuwasil because "we had sworn together and it would be bad if I killed him."

Cases of homicide or assault are often settled by the payment of blood money to the family of the victim. While there is usually negotiation over the exact amount, in no sense is blood money regarded as a substitute for the vindication of the shame of the victim's kinsmen. Blood money is usually only accepted after there has been some attempt, even if unsuccessful, to seek revenge as a means of demonstrating their character as persons of honor.

A basic goal of mediation is to achieve a state of *tabla*, or evenness, in which each party is convinced that the other did not come out ahead in the settlement. This is not easy to achieve. For example, it is felt that if a man's brother is killed, he should take revenge against the killer in such a way that his brother will suffer in the same way. But equivalence of suffering is a very subjective and difficult state to determine and will vary widely with individual interpretation. Mediators must therefore attempt to encourage the acceptance of a more literal and "objective" interpretation of evenness which largely ignores the nebulous question of who suffered more. *Tabla* in a legal sense, therefore, is largely a judgment of evenness made by the mediator and accepted as reasonable by the litigants.

The following case may be cited as an example. Sali and Jirrim killed each other in a fight in which they were the only two persons involved. Consequently it was easy for the *sara* to say that they came out "even," and no further feud developed. But if both Sali and Jirrim had had companions with them, and one of Jirrim's companions had died instead of Jirrim, Sali's kinsmen might attempt to take revenge against Jirrim, saying, "If it were not for Jirrim, Sali would not have died" (that is, Jirrim killed Sali). Thus, while each group lost one man, it might be difficult to make a judgment of evenness. Skilled mediators must confront difficulties such as this.

# A Dyad-Centered Society

The case of Jirrim and Sali brings into focus the whole question of group responsibility in Tausug society. When I first began to work in Jolo, I was predisposed by my training in social anthropology to try to identify an entity anthropologists call "the social structure": the more or less permanent groupings of persons in terms of which day-to-day social life revolves. But it quickly became apparent to me that this was not an easy task in Tausug society. The more I tried to identify permanent features which might set one group off from another, the more confused I became. Rather than permanent groups it seemed as if Tausug society was constantly in flux: communities, households, alliances, mosques, economic groups—everything.

I soon realized that the analysis of social structure in terms of groups was not a profitable way to understand Tausug society. It is not that the Tausug do not conduct many kinds of activities in groups—all societies do that—but that they do not primarily think in terms of a group model of society, and this fact has a very important influence on their actual conduct. Rather than beginning with the idea of a permanent group, the Tausug begin with a dyadic bond between two males and then treat the larger group as an extension of it.

More specifically, Tausug society almost wholly lacks any development of *corporate groups*, a type of association which plays an important role in many societies including our own.[7] A corporate group is essentially a bounded social unit; there are unambiguous ways of telling who is a member and who is not. Ideally it is a perpetual group with continuous recruitment of members; the group continues even though its membership may change. It has fixed ways of choosing leaders, internal solidarity, and a collective will in its various activities (which may be economic, social, or political depending on its purposes). Finally a corporate group is recognized as such within the legal system of the larger society: it can own property and possesses rights and obligations with respect to other groups and the society at large.

There is no group in Tausug society which is fully corporate in the sense above, although the household and the mosque come fairly close, and one might argue that the state as a whole is a corporate group in a certain sense. But for the most part, Tausug groups are defined in terms of their leader rather than by the idea of a permanent group in its own right. The leader organizes the group, or at least activates it for various purposes, rather than being chosen by it. Groups created in this manner tend not to be distinctly bounded, but will vary in their composition with the task at hand. The group has a constant "center" (the leader of an alliance group, the "ego" of a kinship network, the headman of a community, the priest of a mosque), but its composition becomes vague at the periphery. The size of the group depends both on the nature of the task to be accomplished as well as on the influence of the leader; it may vary from a single dyad of two persons to an extremely ramified network of hundreds of persons.

A leader builds up a following by cultivating individual relationships with each of the members of the group. These members in turn may bring their

---

[7] Corporate groups are significant in many African, South Asian, and Near Eastern societies; they are not nearly as important in Southeast Asia, and are almost nonexistent in Filipino social organization (except in a limited legal domain with Western roots). See Lande (1965) for a discussion of the Philippines as a whole. Much of my discussion here is indebted to his analysis.

friends or kinsmen into the network, further increasing the influence of the leader. However, this kind of group cannot last beyond the life of the leader or his ability to hold sway over his followers; it is not always certain that a new leader will necessarily emerge with the same followers. This fact is reflected in the rapidly changing alliance groups constructed for feuding, as well as the more slowly changing boundaries between communities.

An important difference between ego-centered networks and corporate groups is reflected in the fact that benefits from group involvement are expressed by Tausug as highly individual advantages with little emphasis on larger group objectives. Although there is some unanimity of opinion in the minimal alliance group, each participant in a very large alliance has his own private reasons for being there; he has little conception of the group's overall needs. This fact explains why there has been little organized rebellion against Philippine government rule, in spite of the fact that armed Tausug on Jolo outnumber government soldiers by more than 50 to 1. An extended rebellion would require leadership and commitment to generalized ideological objectives, as well as permanent coalitions between the many splinter groups of armed men. But Tausug do not generally fight for generalized objectives unless they have a highly individual relevance for each man. A temporary coalition may be formed against government troops to achieve a highly particular objective, but once each group has achieved its personal goal, it will not interest itself in larger objectives which require delayed gratification. In the nineteenth and early twentieth centuries the ideology of Islam provided a basis for an overall effort against the Spanish and Americans, but the decline of the sultanate has almost eliminated the leadership for this source of unity.

The dyadic stress in Tausug social organization has an important influence on the concept of responsibility in Tausug law: all responsibility is individual, nothing is ever committed in "the name of the group," nor is the group held responsible for what the individual has failed to accomplish. The legal responsibility for a homicide, for example, rests solely with the persons who originally committed it. Ideally one should not seek revenge against a murderer's brother or other kinsmen; no man can really stand in for another man in the redress of a murder. Nevertheless, angry men sometimes do attempt to kill a kinsman of the real murderer, even though it is condemned to do so. But again, this is a question of a difference in perspective between a man's personal desire to achieve an equivalence of suffering (by killing a man's brother you make him suffer as you suffered when he killed your brother) and the more literal idea of equivalence which is recognized by mediators acting within the context of *sara* where this corporate responsibility is not accepted.

## The Traditional State

The sultanate today is only a pale reflection of what it was in the nineteenth century. Yet many features still remain, and it will be useful to describe the

Tausug state as it existed shortly before the American conquest of Jolo Island. I will use the present tense to describe the institutions associated with the sultanate, unless the institution has totally disappeared.

The idea of monarchy among the Tausug is based on a single conception of the ideal correspondence between the microcosm and the macrocosm: just as God governs the universe, so there must also be an earthly head to govern the world. According to the Tausug, the Prophet Mohammed was the sultan in Mecca; the sultanate in Jolo merely continues this tradition. They believe that it is not possible to be a true Moslem without loyalty to a sultan who is compared to God's representative on earth. The sultan possesses *barakat,* a state of religious blessing or grace, which emanates from his person; the ritual kissing of his forehead is compared with kissing the prophet himself and carries religious merit.

But the Tausug conception of the monarchy is quite different from the classic European theory of sovereignty of the seventeenth century. In the Tausug view neither the community nor the sultan is ultimately sovereign. God is sovereign, and the *sara* is sovereign insofar as it does not run contrary to the will of God. Hence the sultanate was not free from dependence on popular will, and as such it cannot be compared to the idea of the divine right of kings. The sultan's judgments—however much they should embody the will of God—are not regarded as infallible; he can commit sins and be condemned to hell the same as any man.

The sultan is thought to be a patrilineal descendant of the Prophet Mohammed. Succession to the sultanate is formally by election, with influential religious leaders, headmen, and royal datus as the electors. The choice is made from a group of close patrilineal kinsmen of the previous sultan, usually his brother, son, or brother's son. However, there is no firmly fixed rule of succession, and disputes over the choice of a new sultan were quite common. A conflict over succession in the 1930s upon the death of Sultan Jamul-ul-Kiram II was never satisfactorily resolved. At present there are two persons who occupy the office, each having influence over roughly one half the island; this is clearly recognized to be an unfortunate situation. Personal charisma and religious devotion are qualities admired in a potential sultan; it is said to be especially important to elect a sultan with a cool temper, for his anger is compared to the wrath of God, and he can easily bring supernatural misfortune upon a man by his intemperate curse.

The sultan is the highest *datu,* the highest religious official, and the highest legal authority. In the nineteenth century he was assisted by a staff of *wajil* (wazir) who were influential local datus and headmen. Each had a special title, and in theory each had a separate function within the state, although in most instances the titles were merely honorific: the *ladja muda* (heir apparent), *ladja laut* (in charge of the navy), the *muluk kahal* (in charge of external war), and several others, including inspector of weights and measures and harbormaster. Each of these officials had a substantial power of base of his own, however, and in no sense did they derive their power solely from the sultan.

There was usually a foreigner (Malayan, Arab, or Bugis) who functioned as the *kadi,* a juridical advisor to the sultan who was learned in the legal theory of al-Shafi'i (an eighth century Near Eastern jurist whose influence is widespread in greater Indonesia). Like all headmen the sultan was surrounded by a group of bodyguards who were younger datus and their followers, called *munari mukahil.* They protected the sultan, collected market fees, occasionally performed executions, and acted as general henchmen. All of the influential datus in the region around the capital, close kinsmen of the sultan, and influential headmen in outlying regions comprise a rather loose representative council called the *duma bissara* (literally "to bring speech"). Ideally, the sultan should consult with this body before undertaking any major affairs of state.

While the Tausug were clearly the dominant group in the sultanate, all ethnic groups in Sulu were included with varying degrees of actual control. The Samals of the various offshore islands, the Yakan of Basilan, and in the eighteenth and early nineteenth century perhaps some of the coastal ethnic groups in North Borneo acknowledged the suzerainty of the Sultan of Sulu.[8] While all aristocrats (datus) were Tausug, appointment to other ranks within the title system were often given to non-Tausug. The sultan had the right to legitimize the position of Samal headmen by appointment to titles in the same manner as he did with Tausug headmen.

Prior to Spanish conquest the capital of the state was usually in Jolo town in western Paticul district, which is today still called by rural Tausug *tiyangi,* or "market," because in the nineteenth century it was the center of external commerce, an entrepot for goods destined for other parts of Southeast Asia and China. After the Spanish conquest of the town the capital was moved to Maimbung on the southern coast. The sultan's palace is built of bamboo and wood in the usual Tausug fashion; it does not have a special style of architecture, although it is considerably larger and has a huge center room for receiving guests, as well as small rooms for wives, children, slaves, and concubines.

Although the Tausug are not a particularly formalistic people, there was more formality and ritual surrounding the sultanate than any other political office. He was addressed in a very circumspect manner using special words used only for the sultan, and usually spoken to only through the use of an intermediary. His followers were obliged to sit at a lower level, and he could not be directly contradicted. Contact with his wives and concubines was forbidden. Only specially appointed persons had the right to wake him up or otherwise disturb him. When he travelled, he was constantly covered by a large state umbrella and was followed by a train of retainers. At the time of his coronation he usually took the name of one of the previous sultans of Sulu in order to enhance the fiction of perfect blood relationship.

An important feature of the Tausug state—which it shares with other "feudal" systems as well—is that it is completely permeated with a legalistic

---

[8] Not surprisingly, however, ethnic groups on the fringes of Tausug control in Borneo also may have given homage to the Sultan of Brunei as well. The boundaries between states in the area were just as vague as the boundaries between communities.

or juridical model of behavior. As we have noted, all officials of the state are juridical officials and representatives of the *sara*, irrespective of whatever other minor functions they may possess. There are no special class of "administrators" devoted to the neutral application of rules of state and wholly dependent on the power base supplied by their employers. There is no autonomous realm of administrative decision; all decisions of the state are cast in a legal mode in which there is constant haggling about claims, rights, and privileges. There are two major functions of the Tausug state: ritual or religious, in which the sultanate is the embodiment of the community of the faithful on earth; and legal, in which the sultanate serves to channel and control conflict.

Any attempt to understand the nature of the Tausug state must take account of one paramount fact: there are no political powers available to the sultan which are not available to a lesser extent to each of the regional and community headmen. While the sultan possesses a religious role and prestige which is denied to lower headmen as the head of a self-defined Islamic state—and this prestige is quite useful in the practical problems of creating and manipulating alliances—, it does not give him any formal political authority which does not have its counterpart on the local level. There is very little differentiation of function in the conduct of political affairs. The sultan can be viewed as an extremely powerful headman, while the local headman might be viewed as a petty sultan in his own domain. The differences between them are not in the types of authority available to them, but rather in the extent and range of that authority.

In order to enforce decisions, the sultan has to depend on the extent and range of his own alliance network, and while all headmen give at least some nominal loyalty to the sultan in an honorific sense, some are clearly more active in their support than others. In the traditional Tausug state, power was more fully concentrated at the bottom of the system—at the community level—and then diffused upward in an ever more precarious system of alliances. It might be possible to describe the Tausug state as a pile of ping-pong balls in which the power of the balls at the top depends on their ability to balance neatly on all the rest. Nevertheless, although raw power or force (the capacity to use violence for legitimate ends) moves upward and ultimately cumulates in the sultanate, the symbols of authority (titles and the power they symbolize) diffuse downward. The sultanate provides the prestige for political authority and delegates this prestige to various local officials, while the local officials in turn give up some of their *de facto* power through support of the sultan.

The sultanate can be described as a *segmentary state* in which there are a number of subunits, or segments, which are not functionally differentiated from each other. There is a centralized government, but there are peripheral points over which the center has little control. Territorial sovereignty is recognized, but it is much stronger at the center than at the edges, shading into more ritual control in the more remote areas. Central and peripheral authorities are mirror images of each other; both have the same rights and obligations vis-à-vis the political system. Thus, in discussing the rights and obligations of the sultan, we would only have to discuss the rights and duties belonging to any office in the realm, perhaps adding some minor footnote to show how the right or obligation was augmented in the instance of the sultan. Briefly, eight primary types of rights, each with corresponding obligations, are associated with political office among the Tausug:

1. *Rights to Perform Legal Functions.* This is the primary emphasis of the system. While a more powerful headman is always in a better position to enforce a decision or handle appeals, there is no differentiation among headmen or sultan with respect to the nature of offenses which can be adjudicated. The sultan has no special powers denied to local headmen.

2. *Rights to Appoint and Regulate Religious Officials.* Appointment of officials rests with the *sara.* In general, lower level officials in a mosque are appointed by the community headman, while the highest leader in each mosque is appointed by the sultan, although in practice the sultan merely legitimizes decisions made on the local level.

3. *Rights to Control Over Territory.* For both sultan and local headman these rights are always greater at the center than at the edges. With respect to the Tausug state as a whole, it is quite unclear where the boundaries were (most of my informants had little comprehension of the question). For example, control over Basilan Island was almost wholly ritual in nature. The Yakan People of Basilan give lip service to the idea of incorporation in the Tausug state, and some religious rituals are given in Tausug, but effective control in any real sense over the interior of Basilan seems to have been very rare.

4. *Control over Subject Peoples.* This right is similar to control over territory. In Tausug theory all subject peoples are "owned" by the sultan, but control over specific groups actually rests with whichever headman is strong enough to extort it. Sometimes this is the sultan himself or his close kinsmen; more commonly it is another influential headman who appropriates this right of the state as his own.

5. *Rights to Wage External War.* Rights to wage external war, including piracy and warfare with Europeans and other indigenous states, resided at all levels of the political system. While the sultan was usually in a better position by virtue of his greater network of alliance to engage in warfare with Europeans, it often happened that local and regional headmen organized piracy missions on their own. While the sultan often signed treaties of various sorts with the Spanish, English, French, and Dutch, he was not always in a position to insure that all his subjects would keep them (Europeans, of course, also broke treaties with the Tausug).

6. *Rights to Tribute and Legal Fees.* While fines and legal fees belong to the *sara,* it is never completely certain to whom these fees will be paid. The percentage reaching the sultan will vary with the situation and the actual configuration of power at the time.

7. *Rights to Control over Markets.* Minor headmen control small tempo-

rary markets, while regional headmen (and today, elected government officials) control permanent regional markets, taking 10 percent of gross sales and gambling revenues. The analogue of these rights for the sultanate was that all of Jolo Island could be considered a market for purposes of trade with Europeans and Chinese. The sultan traditionally had a total monopoly of certain forms of external commerce. He had the right to tax all external trade at 10 percent, although this was subject to negotiation in any given transaction. He also had an exclusive option to trade in certain products which required a centralized point of distribution (although stronger headmen might take these rights for themselves in some cases): bird's nests, pearl, mother-of-pearl, sandalwood, sea-cucumber, camphor, and others. The modes of control which the sultan had over external commerce was substantially the same as the control which local headmen had over markets in their own territory.

8. *Rights to Mediate Private Warfare and Feud.* The sultan's role was to put down internal violence and feuding when it was no longer possible for local and regional headmen to cope with it. He accomplished this by mobilizing alliances with other headmen in distant parts of the realm to counteract violence in another part. Both headmen and sultan had exactly the same relationship to feud within their respective spheres of influence: they mediated between antagonistic segments by throwing their private power to the party with the balance of right. Just as the headman mediated between factions in his own alliance, so the sultan mediated between antagonistic headmen.

# 5

# Folk Islam and the Supernatural

A RECURRING PARADOX in cultural anthropology is the presence of apparently contradictory values and norms in every culture. For the Tausug this paradox is most apparent in the fact that violence is both admired on one level of thought and behavior, and condemned on another. As indicated before, this contradiction involves the presence in Tausug culture of two opposite conceptions of power: secular power and religious power. A man may possess military or political power in the secular world, or religious power in God's world, or neither, but he can seldom possess both at the same time. While the Tausug do not attempt to justify headmanship or military power in religious terms, it is the idea of a universal religious order of mankind based on Islam which has kept the state intact in spite of the almost constant feuding. The divisiveness of secular power is balanced in the long run by the idea of religious unity.

## Spirits, Ghosts, and God

Tausug religion is a folk version of Islam, incorporating most of its major tenets, yet also maintaining many features of ritual and belief which are either survivals of a time when the Tausug were not yet Moslem or else reworkings of orthodox Moslem ideas into a new and unique synthesis. In addition there are numerous religious practices which have little basis in orthodox Islam. These customary practices are usually recognized as such by religious leaders who carefully distinguish them from the purer religious elements. While any religious observance may appear to the outsider to be a seamless whole, priests are able to distinguish between the purely customary and the genuinely Islamic with a fair degree of historical accuracy.

Although God (*Tuhan*) is the ultimate religious concern of the Tausug,

112

much everyday activity is concerned with the propitiation of various lesser spirts who inhabit the forests, treetops, roadcrossings, rocky coasts, and other unusual places. The major class of evil spirits is called *saytan*, but there are also a class of unseen creatures called *jin* which also populate the interstices of the world. The various *jin* are divided into *jin Islam* (Moslem spirits) who do the commandments of God and may occasionally fight the evil spirits, and *jin kapil* (nonbeliever spirits) who violate the commandments of God and may occasionally cause sickness in man.

The various spirits are potentially everywhere, but they are particularly numerous around rocks and trees. One priest told me that originally there was an agreement between the *jin Islam* and the *saytan* that the *saytan* should stay around trees or rocks; otherwise they can be fought by the good spirits and destroyed. Bad spirits are also associated with any place or object which is unusual in any way, such as the parasite belete tree which grows by winding itself around another tree. White warning flags are often placed in spots where spirits are known to live, especially in the rocky barriers along the coasts.

Spirits are said to be responsible for a variety of human woes, especially accidents and sickness. However, they are regarded as a rather stupid lot, easily swayed from their purposes by human ingenuity. They are afraid of all manner of charms and amulets: an unusual shell or rare vine, a recited spell, or a bit of Arabic writing. They can also be held at bay by offerings of food and other gifts. The major method of propitiation, however, is simply to show a certain amount of deference and respect, and avoid hurting their feelings. Before chopping down a tree or otherwise disturbing the natural landscape, most men will address a simple request to the spirit which may live there: "I beg forgiveness from the unseen creatures who may be disturbed by this action."

While the number of unnamed spirits is limitless (they marry and reproduce like man), there are a number of specifically named *saytan* which are widely known for their particular exploits and specialized evil-doing. Spirits are said to reside in especially feared animals, such as large pythons, sharks, and crocodiles. There is the Giant Spirit who falls on people on remote paths and kills them. There is a spirit with the head of a man and the body of a goat. There is a spirit of the forest who can transform himself into a corpse or animal and roll in front of a man causing sickness or death. There is the Owl Spirit who can blind people with its claws.

An important spirit is the *barbalan*, a liver-eating flying creature who thrives on the innards of fresh corpses. Like all spirits, it is rather stupid, and will be frightened simply by a mirror placed on the chest of the corpse. The belief in *barbalan* is interesting because of the manner in which it explains unfortunate physical abnormalities, especially in deaf mutes and persons afflicted with certain birth defects. *Barbalan* are people who involuntarily transform themselves under the influence of a spirit into flying creatures, and can be seen at night as they cross the moon or heard by their distinctive quacking sound. There were two deaf mutes in Tubig Nangka, both living in the same household, who were recognized to be *barbalan.* One admitted to having an involuntary craving for human hearts and livers, and dreaming of flying across the sky. No punishment is ever given these unfortunates because they cannot help themselves, although they will sometimes seek magical cures for their affliction. In great measure the belief in *barbalan* functions to allow deformed persons to assume a role which explains their deformity and makes it appear more natural; it is believed that *barbalan,* like all spirits, were originally created by God so that he could be "complete in Himself."

The closest equivalent to the Christian Devil is the spirit called *Ibiris.* He is the source of all human misdeeds; his purpose is to entice man into doing evil. In Tausug cosmology the human being is composed of four attributes: body, mind, liver, and soul. While different people have different ideas on the subject, evil is usually thought to result from the combination of mind with liver (emotion) under the influence of Ibiris. He is inside all men, but can be resisted by steadfast determination. During prayer, when man's determination to be good is strong, he is thought to leave the body temporarily. When a person dies, the spirit normally leaves the body permanently, but some bad persons are so obsessed by Ibiris that he remains with the decaying body after death, causing it to come out of the grave as a ghost. It roams for 44 days and nights, and finally turns into a pig, dog, or other forbidden animal.

Most Tausug believe in ghosts, although not everyone claims to have seen one. Several times during my stay in Tubig Nangka rumors circulated about ghosts who were said to be making the rounds in the community. A rumor will usually start when someone sees a particular ghost at night, often a recently deceased person who had a questionable reputation during his life, although people are careful about naming specific persons if there is a chance of offending the surviving kinsmen. While ghosts are noxious creatures—decaying flesh surrounded by swarms of flys and maggots—, Tausug are not usually afraid of them. Nor are Tausug normally afraid of the dark, although women are more reluctant to go out alone at night.

# The Curer

A discussion of the belief in spirits leads to a consideration of the role of the curer, or *mangubat,* who is primarily regarded as a specialist in the unseen world of everyday spirits and the problems they bring to man: sickness, ghosts, and the everyday world of common suffering. Strictly speaking, Tausug do not regard the curer as a religious official. In fact there is usually a certain amount of disagreement and competition between the curers and the *agama* religious priests who are really specialists in the problems of the afterworld and do not necessarily concern themselves with lesser spirits. The difference between the two involves the source of knowledge which is employed: Priests derive their knowledge from written and oral traditions which stem directly from God in the form of the

Koran and other holy books, while curers are said to derive their knowledge directly from their intimacy with the offending spirits. Although some priests operate as curers as well, they use a superficially more Islamic style of curing (such as using Arabic-derived spells instead of nonsense spells) and are careful to distinguish their role as priest from their role as curer.

All sickness, accidents, and other misfortunes are thought to be ultimately the will of God who is the source of all power. Nevertheless, many illnesses have an intermediate level of causation embodied in the existence of the various lesser spirits. A person may brush against a fleeting *saytan* and be afflicted by some sickness, or offend a spirit of a tree or rock, or commit some evil act calling for retribution. Spirits are generally said to be involved in sickness when no other normal explanation is readily available: why do some people get tuberculosis while others do not, why does a man go insane, what is the cause of leprosy, why does cholera strike one community but not its neighbor, why does malaria come and go? One man put it quite succinctly when I asked him if leprosy was caused by a *saytan*: "I suppose it is, because we do not know the cause." Spirits are not involved in sickness or misfortune where a normal reason can be identified. Thus, a high fever can be caused directly by brushing against a saytan, but Tausug also recognize that it can be the result of too much time in the sun, with no supernatural explanations required. Similarly, affliction with intestinal worms is not regarded as the result of a spirit, unless it is a very severe case, nor are gunshot wounds thought to be supernaturally inflicted. Belief in spirits as causes of illness supplements common sense as an explanation of disease (although we should remember that common sense in the Tausug theory of disease is not the same as ours).

Individuals who have special knowledge of the ways and customs of the spirits, either because they claim to have direct intimacy with some of them or because they have learned such knowledge secondhand from other curers, may specialize in the curing of illness. Only a small percentage of persons are curers, certainly no more than one in a hundred. They tend to be older people, more often men than women, and usually have a personality which sets them off from the average Tausug, although in varying ways. One man in Tubig Nangka was an extremely flamboyant braggart. Another man in the next community was a rather evil appearing person (both to my eyes and theirs) with an ugly countenance, hard of hearing, and intense beady eyes. Yet another curer was a rather kindly old man who was a deviant only in the sense that he probably was a coward when he was younger. As in many societies, the position of the curer among the Tausug functions to give a meaningful social role to persons who would otherwise seem out of place.

Curing is a private performance; it lacks the public dimensions of common worship which are found in other aspects of Tausug religion. Because it is a private relationship between patient and client, and thought to be of significance only to them and not to the wider community, styles of curing vary considerably with each practitioner. Some make wide use of spells and potions, others use herbs and root medicine. Some read palms, still others typically bathe the patient, while others will order ablutions and ritual acts for the patient to perform. Each curer usually also has a personal pantheon of spirits to whom he will appeal for information which is unknown to other curers; this knowledge is jealously guarded. Sometimes a curer will claim to have a personal guardian spirit who comes to him during his dreams at night and gives information. Commonly curers will keep miniature houses for the saytan to live in, feeding him from time to time. Sometimes curers will claim to marry good spirits in order to acquire information from them about cures.

Most curers began the practice through some unusual occurrence, usually a dream in which they were visited by saytans. One curer in Tubig Nangka acquired his power after he was knocked unconscious in a fight and was visited by a personal guardian spirit. Some curers, however, disclaim any personal intimacy with the spirits, and have acquired their knowledge solely from other persons who have come in contact with spirits.

A person afflicted with an ailment will seek a curer, paying him for services rendered in the form of a small gift of money or perhaps a chicken or some eggs. It is sometimes said that the efficacy of the cure is nullified if a gift is not given. Some curers demand specific fees, although most will accept whatever gift is offered. After diagnosing the disease and identifying the specific spirit causing it, or the specific misdeed of the victim which is causing the ailment, a cure will be prescribed. Various herbs and other medicines are widely used, spells are sometimes employed, or the victim will be asked to make restitution or give redress for some past misdeed. The basic logic of magical curing is usually quite simple; at least the symbolism and logic of Tausug cures are often readily understandable to us. For example, one cure for impotence is to place a six-inch nail in the patients mouth and then drive the nail into a large tree.

Doctors trained in Western medicine practice in Jolo town, and rural Tausug often visit them for serious illnesses. There is little conflict seen between Western medicine and Tausug medicine; in general Tausug admit the superiority of "doctor's cures" for most illnesses, although not denying the strength of their own cures, especially for disease which are thought to have a direct supernatural origin. In addition, many curers have reasonably accurate knowledge of the curing of non supernatural ailments: setting of broken bones, methods of stopping bleeding, and the like.

## Social Organization and Religious Roles

The universalism of Islam exerts considerable influence on the social organization of religion among the Tausug. As a religion Islam aims to embrace all of mankind; Moslems do not think of themselves as belonging to a religion which is restricted to one particular ethnic group, race, or nationality—in theory anybody can get in. This universalism expresses itself at the local level among the

Tausug by the refusal to think of the mosque as exclusively a community or kin-ship institution, although in statistical fact people associate with the mosque where most of their kinsmen and neighbors belong. Furthermore, while each priest is usually tied closely to one particular mosque, he has an informal right to officiate at any other from time to time, especially if he is invited to do so. Priests communicate with each other and are able to travel quite freely, even in cases where their home communities are otherwise feuding. Outside religious leaders are often invited to attend ceremonies in other communities, and in some circumstances, such as a funeral, a traveling official is duty-bound to put aside his other purposes and offer to help.

There are two major kinds of religious buildings: the community mosque and the hamlet chapel. The chapel is a small, semipermanent structure built in areas of high population density which is used mainly for afternoon prayers dur-ing Ramadan—primarily for convenience, since many people do not want to walk as far as a kilometer for afternoon prayers every day. While the chapel is a very in-formal institution, the mosque is defined by more rigid criteria: although it is bamboo, it must be built on a foundation of stone; it must serve an area large enough to attract a large congregation at the Friday prayer; and it must not be within shouting distance of any other mosque. The most important requirement, however, is that a mosque must be built with the permission of the sultan and must be sanctified by inviting the sultan to come and pray in it. Once sanctified, it remains a mosque, including all subsequent buildings placed on the same site.

A person can attend any mosque he wishes. In practice a decision is made by taking into account a number of factors: physical distance from the mosque, loyalty to the headman or religious leaders who control it, kinship and friend-ship relationships with other members, and the absence of personal enemies. Because of the uncompromising universalism of Islam—which the Tausug under-stand quite well—there is no clear sense of membership in one mosque as opposed to any other, although payment of tithes to the mosques' leaders and assistance at the yearly cycle of rituals do indicate some degree of permanence. Normally all persons in the same community will attend the same mosque; in cases where a community is split between two mosques, it usually indicates weak political leadership and a weak sense of community, although physical distance is also a factor. In the region around Tubig Nangka each mosque serves a popu-lation of about 700 persons, although there is considerable variability.

Within the mosque there is a hierarchy of religious officials beginning with the novice rank of *bilal*, the muzzin whose primary function is to call the congregation to attention at the Friday prayer. Upon reaching a certain level of religious learning (as determined by other religious officials, the headman, and general community consensus), the novice will be given the rank of *hatib*, and later, upon further demonstration of competence, the rank of *imam*. The high-est rank is *imam muwallam*; usually there is only one in each mosque, who must be appointed with the approval of the sultan.

In addition to officiating at the Friday prayers, conducting other periodic

*Friday prayer in a rural mosque.*

rituals at the mosque, and assisting the headman in matters of religious law, the priests also preside over a number of individual life crisis rites: births, funerals, weddings, circumcisions, and various individual prayers of thanksgiving which may be offered to mark special occasions. In most communities it is a part-time position which is supported by voluntary contributions for services rendered.

Most priests are ordained during early middle age, although younger men are occasionally ordained as well. While service to God is considered religiously meritorious, there is no special sanctity attached to the role (orthodox Islam actually denies the existence of a formal priesthood with special privileges and powers). They are said to be as likely as any man to be punished in hell for misdeeds, and there is a good bit of joking behind their backs about their personal behavior and occasional inability to live up to the strict precepts laid down for good Moslems. One young man jokingly remarked that if a priest were to encounter a naked girl on a forest path, he would act no differently than any man in that hypothetical situation. And another quipped that perhaps *"alahu akbar"* (God is great) really means "Let us drink coffee" because "they always glance at the coffee in anticipation as they are finishing the prayer."

## The Five Pillars

The core of Islam—in both orthodox theological traditions as well as Tausug folk Islam—lies in the so-called *Runkun Islam Lima*, the Five Pillars of Islam, which is a statement of the bare minimum of belief and ritual obligation. The first pillar is the profession of faith: "There is no God but God, and Mohammed is his prophet." The theological significance of this profession lies in its uncompromising monotheism: the notion that God is indivisible, all-powerful, and all-encompassing. In practice, the belief in lesser creatures such as *jin* and *saytan* does somewhat reduce the impact of this monotheism—in much the same way that the belief in saints does for Christianity , although in no case is the omnipotence of God ever seriously threatened.

The second pillar concerns the faithful performance of the five daily prayers, each occurring at a set time of the day: morning, early afternoon, later afternoon, sunset, evening. Prayer is performed either alone or in a group in special white dress and consists of a set of Arabic phrases which are repeated to a series of various bowings and bodily movements performed while facing Mecca. The primary function of these prayers is to increase the fund of religious merit which is necessary to insure a pleasant afterlife. In practice, only the elderly make the effort to pray five times a day; most Tausug pray only once a week during the communal Friday afternoon prayer in the mosque. In fact, Tausug associate most forms of religious piety with the elderly, and many younger men—especially if they are actively involved in "bad" activities like feuding or piracy—will refrain from keeping religious obligations because it seems somewhat out of character with their current role. They will feel there will be plenty of time when they grow old to concern themselves with the afterlife. Some people even feel that if the young are overly religious, they might shorten their life by accumulating so much religious merit that God will decide to cut it short before they have a chance to do anything bad.

Young women begin to pray only after they are married, while young men may begin after they are circumcised. In the communal Friday prayer, men sit at the front, while women are restricted to the rear, both as a symbolic affirmation of the dominance of men, as well as an assurance that persons of the opposite sex do not accidentally touch each other, thus invalidating the prayer. While the Tausug pray in much the same way as most Moslems, many purely *adat* features have taken root, especially in rural Jolo which has not been subject to recent influence from Egyptian religious teachers. For example, the part of the Friday prayer in Tubig Nangka which calls for the congregation to say "Amin" (signifying the end) is screamed at high pitch specifically as a means of frightening away any spirits which may be hovering nearby. Yet in other communities this practice is not followed; similar variability can be observed in other matters as well.

The third pillar is the fast of Ramadan. During the entire month complete abstinence of all food and drink during daylight hours is required; all eating occurs at night. Almost all Tausug observe the fast during at least some of the twenty-nine days of the month, although only the elderly fast the entire month. The fast is broken at a feast held following a communal prayer in the mosque on the first day of the following month. This day, called *haylaya* (Hari Raya), is time for festivity and merrymaking. People put on their finest clothes and visit each other; there is considerable gambling and feasting; and people from the interior sometimes treat themselves to a visit to the cinema in Jolo town. (Not unexpectedly, westerns and war movies are easily the most popular.)

The fourth pillar is the giving of legal alms, or *jakat*, as a form of tithe to religious officials. In rice-producing areas this is usually computed at 10 percent of all rice harvested, provided the whole harvest is good. There is no means of enforcement; it is believed that to refuse to give *jakat* in a good year will cause a bad harvest in the next. In addition to legal alms, it is also considered meritorious to give *sarraka*, or voluntary alms, to the poor as well as to religious leaders.

The fifth pillar is the pilgrimage to Mecca, which is obligatory only if the person is rich enough to arrange it. Prior to World War II the trip was extremely difficult for Philippine Moslems: the potential pilgrim had to make his way to Singapore or Sumatra and await a pilgrim ship for the Middle East. It usually took more than a year, and often the pilgrim died on route. Today the Philippine government sponsors an annual pilgrim boat, although it has tended in recent years to become a disorganized fiasco in which financial rather than religious motives predominate. Compared to the Tausug, a much greater percentage of Moslems from Mindanao make the trip. Tausug pilgrims consider themselves to be much more pious in their devotion than other Philippine Moslems and seem to be more reluctant to make the trip unless they can do so sincerely.

Very few younger Tausug travel to Mecca, partially because they are less likely to have the money and partially because a pilgrim must assume a markedly different role when he returns. He is expected to be pious, faithful to ritual obligations, and a model of religious conduct. Many young men told me that even if they had the money they would not go on the pilgrimage because when they returned they would have to be "good."

## Pollution and Purification

Tausug folk Islam, in common with many religions which have grown out of the Middle East, is obsessed with a distinction between things which are clean and things which are dirty. While I was able to understand this aspect of their religion intellectually, it was never possible to acquire any real feeling for it.

It is for this reason that I have very little sense of the inner meaning of various religious acts relating to the clean and the unclean. On the one hand, it is possible that the Tausug themselves are completely intellectual in their approach, adhering to the elaborate rules for no better reason than they must in order to remain good Moslems. The prohibition against eating dirty animals like pig is explained simply by saying that God can prohibit anything He wants; it is written and that is that. (In fact, some informants say that pork actually tastes good; God prohibited it so he could serve it as a special reward in heaven!) On the other hand, some ideas about the unclean seem rooted in deep emotional attitudes. For example, the elaborate rules regarding the proper method of bodily elimination seem to be closely related to the Tausug fondness for scatological humor.

A person can be in any of three ritual states: a state of purification, a state of dire ritual uncleanness, or a normal profane state of everyday activity. Ritual purification is necessary before each daily prayer, as well as entrance into any life crisis rite, such as marriage or death. An ablution is performed with clean water to remove ritual and physical impurities, supplemented by spells uttered in Arabic. The state of purity is defiled by any contact with unclean things, falling asleep, or touching the opposite sex.

A person may fall into a state of dire uncleanness by eating a forbidden animal, defecation or urination, sexual intercourse, or contact with menstrual blood, among others. A return to the normal state can be achieved only by washing with pure water and repeating a short prayer.

## Theology and Esoteric Knowledge

In contrast to the variability and idiosyncracies which characterize each curer's method of dealing with unseen spirits, priests strive to maintain a uniformity in ritual and belief based upon the revelations given by God to man and embodied in the Koran. While few Tausug priests can understand Arabic and the bulk of religious learning is transmitted orally, the idea of a written religion is an extremely important Tausug ideal. In Tausug cosmology the truth of Islam is known by man because it was revealed through the Koran, the various holy books, and the teachings of the forebearers. Problems concerning the truth of religion or ritual must always be referred to experts who have the proper knowledge and experience. In no sense can religious truth be found solely by looking inward. Instead of possession *by* God through the passive cultivation of religious sensitivity through meditation, the Tausug stress the possession *of* God through the faithful performance of religious obligations and the accumulation of religious merit through good works and adherence to the Law. Instead of encouraging his followers to understand and accept God inwardly, the Tausug religious leader exhorts them to sincerely follow those God-given rules which will alone lead to rewards in the afterlife.

The Koran embodies the moral law of God. Man cannot make or unmake it; he can only submit himself to it. In Sura 3, verse 5 of the Koran: "It is He who hath sent down to thee the book . . . and the stable in knowledge say 'we believe in it; it is all from our Lord.'" Yet very few Tausug have sufficient knowledge of Arabic to make any immediate use of Islamic writings. For the most part religious leaders rely on oral interpretations supplemented by a few very partial translations into Tausug of some sections of the Koran and other religious writings.

Nevertheless, the recitation and public reading of the Koran in crudely pronounced Arabic is regarded as an act of religious merit; whether it be understood by the reader is of no particular concern. He is thought to participate directly in the truth of the book through the act of reciting it. But inasmuch as this experience is devoid of any meaning outside of itself, it must be interpreted by an expert, one who has been exposed to the oral traditions in terms of which it can be understood. Writing is a kind of magic, one method of gaining power over the living word. This is illustrated dramatically in the practice of writing spells in Arabic and enclosing these written messages in amulets, and in the reluctance to destroy any religious writing in Arabic script. (I once discarded a set of photocopies of a religious text I had been translating, only to discover later that it had been retrieved by a man and hung in his house as an amulet.) It is illustrated in the ritual danger which is said to surround each copy of the Koran: one cannot step over it, place it on the ground, get too near during an oath, and so forth.

Many priests also own esoteric theological books written in very deep Tausug and said to be of considerable antiquity. They deal with such topics as translation of parts of the Koran, the history and origin of the world, the significance of the parts of the human body, the meaning of earthquakes, the significance of many different names of God, how to avoid suffering if one finds himself in Hell, how to conduct certain rituals, questions and answers of the saints to the Prophet Mohammed, and countless similar matters. Many books are concerned with the meaning of symbols and the significance of symbolic permutations: how the major positions of the daily prayer relate to the names of God, how the 7 floors of heaven relate to the parts of the body, and so forth. Much Tausug folk theology is concerned with these numerical permutations: the 7 floors of heaven, the 10 obligations, the 10 prayers of thanksgiving, and 5 (or 7, or 12, or any number, depending on whose treatise is being read) names of God, and so forth. The importance of this esoteric theology for our understanding of Tausug religion lies not in its content—which is immensely variable—, but in its style.

All secret esoteric knowledge which can be used by man to increase his personal power for good or evil is called *ilmu* (Arabic). All *ilmu* comes from

God and is secretly owned by individual men for their personal benefit. It is often inherited from father to son and is regarded as a part of a class of heirloom property which should not be alienated. God created all *ilmu*, both good and evil. He created good *ilmu* in order to help men become good Moslems and proceed in righteous behavior. He created bad *ilmu* which works for antireligious purposes in order to test man's determination to be good.

Much *ilmu* is embodied in semipublic information known mainly to religious leaders. The proper manner of giving rituals and ceremonies, the obligations of man to God, the secrets of the afterworld and man's preparation for it, and other information is largely in the hands of religious specialists, although there is no fixed rule that laymen cannot share in these matters if they wish. In addition to this esoteric knowledge known only to priests, many men also claim access to a more private form of *ilmu* which is jealously guarded. Much of this esoteric knowledge is concerned with methods of avoiding normal ritual obligations of Islam without suffering supernatural consequences. Some men claim, for example, to know secret methods of prolonging life. One of my informants, an extremely agile man who was at least 90 years of age, was widely regarded as the owner of a considerable amount of esoteric knowledge. Most of this was in the form of quasi-Arabic nonsense spells which he inherited from his father and will pass down to his son before he dies.

Some religious leaders, however, do not believe in these methods. There is a noticeable difference of opinion between the priests on some issues, and Tausug do recognize that the interpretations of theological matters will vary. But this is not explained by reference to individual interpretations or idiosyncratic religious experiences; rather, it is viewed as the result of the unequal distribution of knowledge as recorded in books. One priest explained this to me in the following way:

> God originally gave 104 holy books to man. Four were kept by the Prophet for his own use, and 100 were spread around the world. Nowadays there are many different kinds of knowledge because different people have received different books. But the fact that one book is different from another does not mean that He is not perfect. On the contrary, if man only had all the holy books it could be seen that the contradictions were only apparent. Anyway, when we say *alahu akbar* ("God is great") during the daily prayer all of the contradictions are resolved.

## Two Calendrical Rituals

A series of important religious rites are conducted on a yearly calendrical basis, but the Moslem year of 12 lunar months equals only 354 days, so exact comparison with the Western calendar is not possible. On successive Wednesdays in the second month of the year, a special ritual called *pagtulak bala* (literally "to send away evil") is conducted at the beach. This ritual is not derived from orthodox Islam but seems to be based on similar rites common among many non-Islamic peoples of Southesat Asia. It consists of prayers and ablutions conducted in the sea in order to wash away the accumulated *bala*, a kind of supernatural essence of evil which is said to accumulate in the community and the bodies of men. It can manifest itself in many forms: sickness, drought, plague, massive warfare, mischievous spirits. Once a year it must be driven from the land. The entire community assembles at the beach. Prayers are offered by the priests on behalf of the congregation of men, women, and children who wade into the water up to their knees and are doused with sea water. Each person holds a stone in his right hand and tosses it out to sea when the priest is finished with the appropriate spell. The evil is said to be conveyed to the stone and thus permanently expelled from the land. In addition, small rafts are constructed and stocked with aromatic food which attracts mischievous spirits who follow the rafts out to sea, hopefully never to be heard from again. While a few Islamic modernists have tried to discourage this ritual, it is still extremely important. In the town of Jolo, thousands of people gather at the beach for the final Wednesday. It is particularly important for children. My interpreter recalls that as a child he was extremely happy and excited as he threw the stone out to sea, for he knew that all his bad deeds of the previous year were going with it.

In the third month the ritual of *Maulud-al-nabi* is held to celebrate the birth of the prophet Mohammed. Each community mosque chooses one day during the month for this all-night ritual which consists of continuous Arabic chanting from traditional holy books by the priests. Special flowers are placed in the center of the mosque which symbolize the Prophet (see photograph on page 125) and when a certain section of the chanting is reached about midway each person in the mosque stands and holds one of the flowers. This act increases the fund of religious merit of the participant, and is the only part of the total ritual which involves the congregation in any active manner. As in many Tausug ceremonies, the priests conduct the affair on behalf of the audience who on their part seem unconcerned with what the priests are actually doing; after all, it is they who have the expertise. The audience sits gossiping, joking, smoking, and talking of less pious matters. About midnight a communal feast will be held in the mosque. Sharing food with others is a meritorious act, and each family will bring a tray filled with feast food: mounds of rice topped with hardboiled eggs covered with coconut, fried fish, vegetables, beef, rice cakes, and sweets. The whole point of the feast, however, is that each family eats someone else's food in order that all may be credited with generosity.

## Birth and Circumcision

During labor a woman is assisted by female kinsmen and friends as well as one or more older women who act as midwives. The midwife is actually con-

*Maulud-al-Nahi: all night ceremony in honor of the Prophet's birthday.*

sidered to be a religious official in her own right who has knowledge in religious matters pertaining solely to women. Men are excluded from the house while a woman is in labor; the husband remains outside on the porch waiting the good news so he can fire his rifle to announce the birth—a few shots if it is a girl, even more if it is a boy. He may also busy himself with practical matters such as gathering firewood or fetching water. After the birth the placenta is placed in a green coconut shell and will later be "planted" in the ground during a full moon—it is said to be still alive.

The child is seldom named immediately. The parents may decide on a temporary name after a few days, but if the child is sickly, it will be changed until a lucky one is found. Names are sometimes based on Arabic names in the Koran, well-known Americans (Jefferson, Pershing), or nonsense words which are chosen merely because they sound good. Each person has only one first name, in addition to a last name consisting of his father's first name.

Within the child's first year it will have its hair cut for the first time in a ritual called *paggunting*. The hair is moistened with a bit of coconut water, oil, and sugar, and a lock of freshly cut hair is placed inside a green coconut which is hung over a path leading to the house. One informant interpreted the ceremony as necessary to remove the excess semen which may have stuck to the child's hair during birth, although others were skeptical of this explanation. The parents may also give a large feast for kinsmen and friends at this time.

At the same time a ceremonial "weighing" of the child may be given in fulfillment of a solemn promise made to God on the occasion of its birth. Parents and kinsmen prepare brightly colored cloth bags of rice and other gifts which are tied to one end of a strong bamboo pole suspended from the rafters. The child is laid in a cloth seat and suspended from the other end of the pole in order to balance the rice, and is rocked up and down while priests conduct a brief ritual and chant in Arabic. After the ceremony the rice is given to the priests as alms, adding to the religious merit of the child. A ritual weighing can also be given on behalf of any person who wishes to thank God for good fortune. On one occasion a 200-pound young man was balanced against his weight in rice because he had been captured by the Constabulary and his father made a solemn promise to God that if he was released he would conduct the ceremony.

At some time before puberty the child will be given a blood sacrifice in his name, usually on the occasion of the slaughtering of an ox or water buffalo for some other social event. The soul of the animal will be beseeched to bear witness in heaven to the fact that the child is the offspring of his true parents. Without this sacrifice, it is said that he would not recognize his own parents in the afterlife.

Sometimes before puberty, usually at around age 10, a boy will be circumcised. The Tausug place great importance on circumcision as a symbol of Islam, claiming that a person cannot be a real Moslem without it. It has assumed an importance far greater than usually found in the Middle East; almost assuming the status among the Tausug as an additional "pillar" of Islam.

The brief religious ritual is conducted by one of the few priests who also has the necessary surgical skill. Circumcision is a private ceremony; if the boy is old enough, he may arrange to have it done on his own. The operation is fairly painful, although it is considered bad form to cry, and as far as I can tell most boys are rather stoical about it. A comparable ceremony for girls involving a very light scraping of the clitoris is conducted by the midwife when the girl is about four. Both ceremonies are simply called *pagislam*, meaning "to make a person a Moslem." They have no other purpose, although it is sometimes claimed that sexual satisfaction is increased.

Many boys and girls begin to study the Koran at seven or eight years of age, learning to pronounce the Arabic characters and read in Tausug. Teachers are usually poorer women who give lessons to supplement their income. More girls than boys complete the training, partially because reading the Koran at funerals is a woman's specialty, and partially because boys are less likely to put

*First public recitation of the Koran by children who have attended Islamic school.*

up with having their knuckles rapped if they make a mistake in the rote learning. When the child has mastered the technique of reading, his parents will usually have a "graduation" ceremony in which the child demonstrates his knowledge before assembled guests in a formal social occasion (see photograph above).

## Fate and Luck

Everyday conversation among the Tausug is rich in reference to the inevitability of fate and luck; by all standards the Tausug are a extremely fatalistic people. They strongly believe in the inevitability of events as determined by agents and forces beyond the common-sensical control of the individual. Yet fatalism among the Tausug does not lead to a cozy quietism or a doctrine of despair which saps individual responsibility. Unless the individual ego is denied in the face of the world (and we have seen that the Tausug are a markedly individualistic people), a belief in fate does not necessarily lead to passivity. For the Tausug the acceptance of fate enhances a man's justification for action in the world rather than diminishing it. The adventure and risk seeking which are so important a part of their life style derive their meaning from the ultimate fate-fulness of the world: if it is predetermined that a man must die, then he might as well fashion his death as part of an adventure.

While all fate comes from the will of God, Tausug distinguish between two kinds of fate: theological fate and empirical fate. Theological fate, or *kadal*, is the singular fate of the individual, the reality of his own death. *Kadal* derives its meaning from the whole system of religious belief and the theology of the afterlife. A man's *kadal* is predetermined by God and completely un-avoidable. God has made a promise to each man concerning the time, place, and conditions of his death, and this fate is permanently attached to his soul. The idea of *kadal* is the means by which Tausug give a name to the reality of suffering, and in so doing learn to live with it. As one man put it:

> Every man must die, but there are various roads to death which are determined by God and cannot be changed. There is the road of death through sickness, or falling, or drowning, or poisoning, or childbirth, or through warfare. These things are a part of his *kadal*. When a child is born, there is *kadal* in his closed fist. When he opens it for the first time, his *kadal* goes to God and it returns to him only when he is about to die. God has made a promise to every individual when he will die. When the promise is combined wiht our *kadal*, then we will die and there is nothing which can be done to change this. We cannot avoid it, but we may predict it if we have the right divination.

Empirical fate, or luck, is called *sukud*. It is the causal explanation of phenomena which occur for no comprehensible reason: why does a man fall down his house ladder and break a leg, why do some people have better coconut harvests than others, why do some people win a gambling, why do the rich prosper, and so forth? Such luck is predictable through the proper use of fortune-telling books and other devices. It attaches itself to man's body, not his soul. It is profane, and unlike *kadal*, does not relate to a larger system of religious belief.

Both fate and luck refer to those acts of man which are outside the realm of human intention, which are beyond the ability of man to control his own destiny. To be cursed for falsely swearing on the Koran is not bad luck be-cause the cause was surely a work of individual will. To gain riches through hard work is not good luck in itself. To be hit by bullets and still live is the result of good amulets, not good luck.

## Death and the Afterlife

The Tausug approach to death and the afterlife revolves around the con-cept of religious merit and its acquisition by man through the accumulation of good deeds and regular performance of ritual obligations. Religious merit has both an active and a passive dimension. As the result of man's active striving to acquire merit, it is called *karayawan*, literally "goodness." As a gift of God to man according to principles which only He can ultimately understand, it is called *pahala* (the passive dimension). In addition, *karayawan* in this context also implies a state of pleasure and happiness in the afterlife. Many of my informants explained the idea to me by describing heaven as analogous to a state of perpetual sexual orgasm. But the amount of *karayawan* one receives in heaven is directly proportional to the amount of *pahala* one has been given by God in return for good deeds.

For the Tausug heaven and hell are thought of less as physical places than particular states of being. *Sulga* (heaven) and *narka* (hell) are commonly used terms derived from Arabic, but quite often *karayawan* (state of goodness) and *kasiksaan* (state of suffering) are used instead. The pleasures of heaven and the pains of hell—which are vividly described in the Koran—are a source of much everyday imagery. One old man told me of two dreams during which his soul visited heaven briefly before returning to his sleeping body. In the first dream he went to heaven and saw his recently murdered son, sitting in a golden rocking chair and surrounded by beautiful women, food, and other pleasures. He was about to enter when his son said "Do not come in father . . . it will be a long time yet until you die." In the second dream he came to a bridge leading to the entrance to heaven crossing over a pit of fire. He saw that one of his distant kinsmen had fallen from the bridge and was being devoured by a crocodile as punishment for stealing a lantern from the mosque. Another woman was being punished for inducing an abortion: she had fallen into the fire, and a monkey was tugging ferociously at a bamboo tree which had sprouted from her vagina. A rapist was watching his penis being cut off; a blasphemer was having his tongue pulled out; and thieves were dragging their stolen goods through the fire. He was scared as he approached the bridge, but a helpful man told him to read the Koran. As he crossed he looked back to see many screaming people falling into the fire.

The Tausug conception of the afterlife is a mixture of orthodox Moslem ideas syncretized with older ideas common to many of the non-Moslem peoples of the greater Indonesian Archipelago, especially the idea of multiple souls. While no two religious leaders have exactly the same ideas of the subject, the theory of the afterlife described by one young religious leader can be taken as fairly typical. According to this man, the human person is divided into body and soul. The body is composed of proportions of the four cardinal elements: earth, air, fire and water; in addition, the body possesses the faculties of intelligence and feeling. Since the state of *karayawan* is primarily a sentient state, it follows that the religious merit given by God to man is attached solely to the body, not the soul. Only the body is capable of the free choice which leads to good or evil; the soul is good from the beginning.

The soul itself is actually composed of four souls. First is the transcendental soul which exists in heaven at all times, although it will occasionally visit the body when it is praying. God created one transcendental soul for each person, past, present, and future. It is totally good, does not suffer the punishments given to the body, and will eventually be reunited with the body in heaven. Second, there is the life-soul, sometimes associated with the blood. Before a child is born, it begins to attach itself permanently to his body, imperfectly at first, and does not leave until he dies, although it may wander during dreams. Third, there is breath, the real essence of life itself, which always remains while the person is alive, even while the life-soul may be temporarily gone. Finally, there is the spirit-soul which also wanders during dreams and which is the essence of a man's shadow.

When a man dies, all four souls are initially separated from his body. Since the source of all sin is the body and since all men have committed some evil deeds during their life, the bodies of all men (with the exception of a very few extremely pious individuals) go to hell. The time spent being tortured in hell varies with the number of bad deeds which have been recorded.

Eventually the ashes of the body leave hell and are sifted to separate the remaining good from the bad. The good goes to heaven and is reunited with the soul. The amount of pleasure felt by the body in heaven is proportional to the amount of good works the individual has performed in his lifetime. All Moslems eventually reach heaven, while Christian Filipinos are destined to remain in hell forever. Americans, according to one informant who was perhaps being tactful, go to an intermediate state between heaven and hell.

Once religious merit is acquired by an individual, God will not take it away again. Good behavior is always eventually rewarded, and bad behavior punished in a relatively direct and uncomplicated manner. There is little emphasis on faith, devotion, grace, or forgiveness, although similar ideas are not unknown to the Tausug.

One of the major differences between Tausug folk Islam and the stricter Islam taught by the Egyptian religious teachers in Jolo concerns the transference of religious merit from one individual to another. According to the Tausug, if one man is innocently killed or otherwise victimized by another, the accumulated religious merit of the killer is transferred to the victim, while the accumulated bad deeds of the victim are transferred to the killer. The uneven exchange of life is balanced by a compensating exchange of religious status in the afterlife; reciprocity in this world is balanced by a complementary reciprocity in the other world. Most Tausug fighters believe that if they die in battle they will be automatically "inside of *karayawan.*" These ideas are opposed by the foreign teachers, but given the great emphasis which Tausug place upon reciprocity and exchange in all aspects of their life, it is understandable that they are applied to religion as well.

When death comes, there is no public expression of grief on the part of kinsmen and friends; whatever people may feel in private, the acceptance of inevitable fate dominates the public aspects of Tausug funerals. There may be some crying on the part of close consanguine kin, but it is thought better not to do so. The only overt expression I observed of strong grief on the part of a male was a young father who began raving and aimlessly firing his rifle shortly after his three year old son died of dysentery. In cases of homicide the grief of the victim's close kin is usually hidden by sentiments of vengeance directed against the killer.

The body is taken immediately to the home of the deceased or the home of close kin. The body is thought to be both physically and ritually polluting and must be thoroughly cleansed by religious officials before internment through a series of bathings in ritually prepared water. Defecation must be removed from the anus, body orifices cleaned and plugged with cotton, and the body dressed in a loosely fitting white shroud.

On the evening before burial, ritual prayers are offered in Arabic for the deceased. Young women who are expert in reading the Koran are invited to read in an effort to increase the fund of religious merit and ease the pains of hell. The object of the recitation is to finish as much of the Koran as possible in one evening, and each woman begins reading in a different place at the same time in a deafening torrent of ritual chant. One week after the death a special seventh-day ceremony is held by the kinsmen of the deceased. A major feast is given and a prayer is offered for the dead. As on all social occasions of this kind, distant kinsmen, friends, and allies are invited and contribute to the cost of the occasion.

Burial usually takes place the afternoon following the day of death. A final version of the normal daily prayer is done on behalf of the dead by the priests. The body is carried down from the house on a bamboo stretcher and conveyed to the nearest cemetery where a grave has been prepared by hollowing out a niche in the earth from the sides of a pit. The body is placed facing Mecca, the niche is boarded up, and the pit filled with dirt.

Tausug believe that it is not merely being dead which is significant, but being dead and knowing it. Since the corpse is not totally devoid of feeling, it must be told that it is dead so that it will not persist in the delusion that it is merely dreaming. At the graveside a special ritual is read in Arabic, which is necessary in order to wake the dead up, tell him he is dead, and allow him to become adjusted to his new status. If this is not done properly the wandering soul of the dead will perhaps communicate with the living through dreams.

While in everyday behavior Tausug are quite unconcerned with the souls of the dead, two yearly rituals are conducted in each community to pacify them. In the month prior to Ramadan the ritual of *nispu* is held in the mosque on the full moon. A feast is given and prayers are offered on behalf of the souls in heaven and hell; if this was not done, it is said that the dead would curse the living. The souls are attracted by the smell of the food, and some people say that they also partake in the feast. Several days later the entire community turns out to the cemetery to clean the graves, remove weeds, and plant flowers. A prayer for the dead is offered by religious leaders, and the Koran is briefly read on each to ease the sufferings of the deceased and bring religious merit to the reader. This is followed by a communal feast in the graveyard.

Social anthropologists sometimes maintain that the religion of a society is a reflection of its social structure, that the ideas men have about life influence the ideas they have about death. Most Tausug believe that the fate of a man's body and soul in the afterlife depend at least partially on how well his surviving kinsmen perform the rituals on his behalf: prayers, reading the Koran, pouring water on the grave "to cool the body off," repeating the profession of faith over and over again, and others. Again the Egyptian teachers disagree, but they have had little success in changing belief outside the town. In a society where a man's death may often be the result of his obligations to his kinsmen and friends, it seems reasonable that these same kinsmen should be able to help him in turn after his death.

Another source of disagreement between traditional Tausug and the small percentage of Islamic modernists in the town concerns the importance given to private magic and esoteric knowledge as a means of obtaining a shortcut into heaven, bypassing the usual good works and ritual obligations. As indicated before, Tausug set very high ethical standards for themselves, yet consistently violate these standards in practice. The reason for this is partially a result of the same tendencies toward risk taking and stress seeking which operate in piracy and feuding. Just as a man can take a physical risk involving danger to his body, so he can also take an ethical risk involving exposure to the dangers of the afterlife and a punishing God. But the risk, like the risk of armed combat, is not "really" a risk if the person has the proper magical knowledge. It is for this reason that to an outsider it often seems as if the Tausug throw themselves into evil with a robust enthusiasm, and then regret their conduct later with as much enthusiasm, especially as they grow older and begin to see a day of reckoning. Tausug folk Islam is, perhaps, a form of adventure for the elderly.

## Ritual Suicide and the Changing View of Christians

While Islam probably had begun to penetrate the southern Philippines several hundred years before the Spanish arrived, much of the religious history of Jolo since the sixteenth century was profoundly influenced by the continuous warfare between the Tausug and the Spanish. Faced with an ethnocentric and militant Christian missionary zeal to the north, the Tausug conception of Islam grew naturally to emphasize the militancy of the holy war, or *jihad*, against non-believers.

Group resistance against the Spanish prior to the middle of the nineteenth century was relatively well organized through the institutions of the sultanante. But with the Spanish conquest of Jolo town in 1878 responsibility for the *jihad* came increasingly to be a concern of the individual. The institution of the personal *jihad*, called *pagsabbil* by the Tausug and *juramentado* by the Spanish, was a form of ritual suicide in which a man went to a Christian settlement and began killing more or less indiscriminantly until he in turn was killed. A man knew it was certain death, but the goal was to bring as many non-Moslems with him as possible. On occasion, large groups committed suicide together in the form of a battle against Christians in which their total slaughter was assured. On other occasions, primarily in the early American period, large numbers of Tausug gathered together in a stone fort and awaited attack, fighting to the death.

A person who decided to commit suicide was required to ask permission of the headman, his close kinsmen, and sometimes the sultan. He was given all the rituals of final burial (washing, prayers, purification) while he was still alive; the body would not be recovered and it was necessary to insure that it was prepared to enter paradise. The hair was shaved, the eyebrows plucked, and the penis bound in an upright position in order to insure that he would remain upright and not fall. Special magic would be learned in order to make the person brave. On the morning of the appointed day he would make his way to a Christian settlement (usually Jolo town or Zamboanga), gain entrance to the market, and begin killing with his *kris*. Killing was quite selective: Moslems were excluded if known, and women and children were sometimes spared. The goal was to kill Christian males, preferably soldiers. Since the person was in a complete frenzy of rage, it was sometimes possible for him to dispatch several persons before being brought down.

The conduct of ritual suicide was based on the belief discussed in the last section: that an innocent death brings religious merit to the victim. Since all Christians (particularly the Spanish) were defined as evil, any death at their hands was by definition an innocent death and hence religiously meritorious. The purpose of ritual suicide was not so much to kill Christians as to be killed by them, thus insuring an immediate entrance into paradise. The person who was victimized was snatched up after death by a white horse and conveyed immediately to heaven where his pleasures were multiplied sevenfold, without having first to go to hell.

Ritual suicide in its traditional form is no longer practiced, although all of the basic beliefs are still accepted. The decline is partially due to the decrease in the number of outgroups which are considered sufficiently evil to meet the requirements of the institution. As Americans and Filipinos came to be better liked, they could no longer be killed. Furthermore, the practice was always directed against non-Moslems who were as a group military enemies of the Tausug. During World War II it was sometimes directed against the Japanese, although it was never done to the Chinese or other non-Moslems who did not represent any threat to the Tausug. Today suicide is conducted only against members of the Philippine armed forces; an innocent death at the hands of the army is said to make the victim *sabbil*, entitling him to an immediate place in heaven.

Traditional ritual suicide has also partially declined because of the decreasing capacity of headmen to command sufficient force to enforce public executions for major crimes. While headmen never had the right to require a person to kill himself, a man accused of a serious religious crime might voluntarily decide to commit suicide rather than submit himself to the law.

While the Tausug are still intensely ethnocentric in matters religious, the association of religious opposition with political opposition and warfare is waning. This is perhaps best illustrated in changes in ritual which have occurred in Jolo during the last 20 years. For example, certain ritual features which are symbolic of the war against Filipinos have disappeared from the Friday prayer at Jolo, but are still practiced in the relatively isolated island of Pata to the south. The conduct of the priest during the "sermon" is described in my notes as follows:

> The priest who is to read the sermon removed his prayer garments and was dressed in everyday clothes. A piece of white cloth was tied on his head while another repeated an Arabic incantation in order to invoke the Prophet. He then was given a kris (for his right hand) and a spear (for his left hand). The other priest held the book while he read the sermon. At no time did any of the congregation raise their eyes to look at him, but when the reading was finished they rushed up together in a mad scramble to be the first to kiss his forehead.

Informants saw this ritual as symbolic of the war against the Filipinos. The priest literally becomes the Prophet during the reading, and nobody can look at him without danger. The Prophet leaves immediately after the reading, so it is necessary to be quick if one wishes to acquire religious merit in the act of kissing his forehead. The kris and the spear symbolize that the Prophet is fighting against the Filipinos and Spanish.

The ritual use of spears and krisses in the Friday prayer is no longer found in the main island of Jolo. Many religious leaders feel that the ritual is outmoded, for as one remarked, "We stopped doing it that way some time ago because we are no longer fighting against the Christians—the war is over now."

# 6

# The Tausug
# and the Modern Philippines

THE TAUSUG, along with several other ethnic minorities in the Philippines, are a small outpost of Islam in a sea of Christianity. At the time of the creation of the Philippine Commonwealth in 1935, many Moslem leaders in the Philippines favored continued administration by the United States rather than union with a feared Philippine nation dominated by non-Moslems. While such sentiment still exists in some parts—a question I was constantly asked by rural folk was "When are the Americans coming back?"—most realistic leaders realize today that their future is firmly wedded to the Philippine Republic. While the last few years have seen several attempts to create a Pan-Islamic political movement in the southern Philippines, usually under Magindanao leadership but occasionally involving Tausug as well, these movements have lacked much grassroots support and have served primarily to call attention to the neglect of the Moslem areas by the national government and to extract concessions from the government on behalf of local leaders. Educated Tausug and other Philippine Moslem leaders realize quite clearly that their own political futures are much more secure within the Philippine national setting than would be true if a serious attempt were made for independence or affiliation with Malaysia. Some rural Tausug agree that ideally affiliation with a Moslem nation such as Malaysia or Indonesia might be preferable, but without leadership this very vaguely formed ideology is not easily transformed into concrete political action.

Unless a major political crisis or even civil war envelops the Christian Philippines, the Tausug will continue to be an official part of the Philippine Republic for the foreseeable future. Nevertheless, it is only the commitment of the educated Tausug leadership which keeps the ties to Manila as strong as they have been. Rural Tausug, for the most part, have only a very hazy idea of the meaning of the Philippine national government. For example, nobody in Tubig Nangka, except the headman's son who had been to government grammar

135

school, knew the Philippine national anthem, and all felt that they were primarily Tausug, not Filipinos.

There are grammar schools covering the first few grades within reach of most rural areas; about one-half of the children of Tubig Nangka had been at least to second grade at the time I was there. But the official curriculum (which is largely determined in Manila) is irrelevant to the realities of everyday life, and the teachers, who are usually educated Tausug, themselves have only a partial understanding of the meaning of a modern nation-state. There are advanced elementary schools in the municipal centers for children whose parents can afford to send them, and public and private high schools in Jolo town. Two colleges—one Moslem and one Christian—also operate in the town, primarily graduating teachers and aspiring civil servants. Few lines of work other than teaching or other government service are available in Sulu to those educated beyond grammar school. Since Tausug are very reluctant to migrate outside of Sulu, there is a growing glut of unemployed young people who have been to school and then find themselves neither able to obtain suitable employment, nor satisfied to return to the rural life of their parents.

At present the major concern of the national government with Jolo is the so-called "peace and order" problem. Judged from the perspective of a government official, rural Jolo has some of the worst law and order conditions to be found in the country, and probably the highest homicide rate. So-called "outlaw bands"—which I have named minimal alliance groups in this book—are often luridly described in Manila newspapers as the root of the law and order problems, yet they are composed of very intelligent and friendly young men who in many ways are the cream of their society. In short, much of the relationship between the Tausug and the national government is characterized by the grossest kind of misunderstanding and misinformation.

For the most part, the Tausug have adapted quite well to some of the major features of the Philippine political system. Dyadic ties and constantly changing factionalism are as much a feature of domestic politics among Christian Filipinos as they are among the Tausug, and this similarity has facilitated Tausug acceptance of some of the more superficial features of the Philippine political process. Yet the Tausug have been most reluctant to accept Philippine law and legal process; and understandable refusal in the light of the primacy which Islam places upon law.

The first question which must be asked about the government's law and order problem on Jolo is "Out of whose law?" While the traditional Tausug legal system has undergone many changes with the decline of the sultanate and with the increase of firearms since the end of World War II, it is still a reasonably effective instrument of justice in most rural areas. Because traditional ideas about land tenure have become somewhat outmoded with increasing commercial coconut production, the only Philippine law which is even partially accepted by rural Tausug is land law. Land conflicts are still largely solved by mediation, however, if only because the presence of firearms makes mediation the only sensible way of solving them. If Philippine land law were strictly enforced—especially where absentee titleholders own huge tracts of land because of irregularities in the survey procedure—, problems of land tenure might arise where none existed before. As long as every man has a gun in his house and power is relatively decentralized, genuine exploitation of tenants is impossible.

The Philippine government operates branch offices in Jolo of most of the various national bureaucracies: customs, internal revenue, immigration, motor vehicles, highways, aviation, agriculture, health, post office, antismuggling police, education, and numerous others. But apart from the public schools and occasional health and agriculture services, the average rural Tausug has contact with the Philippine government primarily through local elected officials, the Philippine Constabulary, and Philippine judges. There are seven municipalities (roughly "counties") in the government administration on Jolo Island. Each has a series of locally elected leaders, usually Westernized Tausug: mayor (*mayul*), vice-mayor, councilmen (*conseyul*), and barrio or local leaders (*capitan barayu*). Barrio captains tend to be local headmen in the traditional system who have acquired the new title. Mayors, on the other hand, tend to be ambitious and upwardly mobile politicians who desire to acquire power in non traditional ways, although they are often called to perform traditional functions which once belonged to higher regional headmen. Their primary function, however, vis-à-vis rural Tausug, is to serve as a buffer between their followers and the larger provincial and national government, mainly its legal institutions. Rural Tausug do not look upon their elected officials primarily as administrators, but rather as legal officials of a special sort. Many Tausug feel that the possession of an elected title such as mayor or councilman entitles the holder to act as *sara*, although there is some disagreement whether this applies to *sara agama* (religious law) or merely *sara upis* ("law of the office," government law). Nevertheless, elected officials, both municipal and provincial, are often involved in the mediation of serious feuds, usually cooperating with traditional leaders.

Relative to the size of the province, the Philippine Constabulary (domestic army) on Jolo is the largest command in the country. Its primary function is to insure law and order and arrest persons accused of crime in government courts. This is an impossible task, both because the numbers of men required to accomplish it would be prohibitive and because there is very little civilian cooperation. The Constabulary is looked upon largely as an occupying army, and its effective control over the hinterland of Jolo seldom extends further than the barbed wire surrounding its various headquarters. Furthermore, assignment to Sulu is regarded—whether officially or unofficially—as a punishment for the poorer quality officers and men. It is one of the toughest assignments in the nation, and before World War II only the finest officers and men were sent to Jolo; today this situation has been largely reversed. Rural Tausug quite often suffer various abuses at the hands of the Constabulary enlisted men, although commissioned officers are seldom directly involved. One of the reasons Tausug seldom surrender to the Constabulary in battle is a fear—which was expressed to me by several men—that they will never teach the town alive. This fear is probably exaggerated, but it illustrates the extremely low level of trust between the Constabulary and the Tausug.

For the most part, however, the ongoing conflict between the Tausug and the Constabulary is largely a stand-off. The Constabulary has greater firepower, but the Tausug have greater mobility and the advantage of greater familiarity with guerilla tactics. As a result, the only way the Constabulary is able to defeat an armed "outlaw band" is to cultivate an alliance with another band who are enemies of the first, an ironic situation in which government forces are drawn into the very social system which they are supposed to eliminate.

One of the primary concerns of the Constabulary is the collection of un-licensed firearms (less than 5 percent of the firearms in Sulu are licensed), an impossible task which periodically generates a concerted crackdown by the gov-ernment, always ending in failure. A massive military operation on Jolo simply cannot work, for unless the government wishes to commit itself to a permanent garrison of tens of thousands of men, sooner or later the soldiers must leave and the situation will return to the way it was before. The government attempted a massive military operation in eastern Jolo in the early 1950s against an "outlaw" named Kamlun, and in certain regions almost all men of fighting age were killed. Their children are now grown men lacking mature adult leadership, and at the time I left, a potentially explosive situation was brewing in this area. The ideas men have about law and justice cannot be eliminated by force without destroying the entire society.

The crux of the entire problem of the relationship between rural Tausug and the Philippine government lies in the conflict of legal institutions; relations with the Constabulary and the need for economic development in the province are minor compared with the need for legal accomodation. The average Tausug man in most rural areas would rather die than submit himself to Philippine jus-tice. First, he does not understand it. Second, he knows that money for lawyers, court fees, and occasional bribes is very expensive, and he would rather invest his money in guns and ammunition. Third, he often mistrusts lawyers. Fourth, he knows that he may languish in jail for many months before trial. Fifth, he knows that the power of the Constabulary to capture him is very slight. Sixth, he knows that only the poor and the powerless go to jail. If he is guilty, he will not surrender; if he is innocent, he is insulted that the government has accused him.

However, rural Tausug are very pragmatic in their approach to the system of Philippine justice and make use of Philippine courts when it suits their purpose to do so. But for the most part a rural Tausug goes to a govern-ment court in order to further his dispute, not to settle it. Typically, if a man has an enemy he will try to convince the municipal judge to sign a warrant of arrest against him, thus insuring that the Philippine Constabulary will also be looking for him. He may even attempt to help the Constabulary locate and capture his enemy. Similarly, by making use of alliances with politicians with influence over the government legal process, he will try to keep warrants of arrest from being issued against himself. Thus, it might be said that enemies use warrants of arrest against each other in somewhat the same way as they use bullets. This situation easily gets out of hand as far as the Constabulary is concerned. In 1968 there were about 500 outstanding warrants in Luuk municipality for a population of about 35,000. Taking into account women and children and the fact that each "outlaw" will have numerous kinsmen who will assist him, the Constabulary is faced with the awesome task of fighting at least a third of the adult male population at any one time.

Very few of these warrants are ever cleared through normal Philippine court channels. Conflicts—including homicide—are usually settled out of court by traditional means, and the government prosecutor usually finds that all his witnesses refuse to testify. Only a very small percentage of persons accused of murder are captured, even fewer are ever brought to trial, and most cases are eventually dismissed for lack of evidence. Over a five-year period in Luuk municipality, only two persons were sentenced to jail for murder—these were both poor and powerless persons—in spite of the fact that there were well over 200 killings during that time. The Philippine system of justice simply does not work in Jolo except as an unwitting supplement to traditional Tausug system of revenge.

In some very large feuds involving hundreds of participants and many warrants of arrests, an informal agreement will often be worked out among the principals to the feud, political leaders, the municipal judges, prosecuting attorney, as well as the Constabulary, in which the feud will be settled by traditional means. Then all warrants of arrest will be dropped in return for the surrender of several firearms to the Constabulary. Two years before my stay in Tubig Nangka, almost every adult male in the community was under warrant of arrest in connection with a feud in which their enemies were able to obtain the favor of the government judge. When the case was finally mediated, all the warrants were erased. Conflict between the Constabulary and rural Tausug, sometimes involving large battles, usually revolves around the attempts of the Constabulary to enforce warrants of arrest or collect unlicensed firearms.

Tausug sometimes use government law as a means of obtaining redress for offenses which do not really exist in Tausug law. An outraged father will occasionally cynically charge his daughter's abductor in the government courts with kidnapping, as a means of forcing the young man to pay a higher bride-wealth. Or a jealous first wife will sometimes charge her husband with bigamy, in spite of the fact that plural marriages are sanctioned in Tausug law. By playing off one system against the other, some persons are able to obtain advantages they might not otherwise receive.

The Tausug are not alone in facing this conflict between traditional common law and Philippine government law; it is a problem among all of the cultural minorities in the Philippines. However, for many of the minorities there is no alternative except forcible acceptance of Philippine law, especially if they are small and surrounded by Christian settlers.

This is not the case in rural Jolo. Tausug are completely in control of their own island, extremely well armed, and in no mood to be pushed around. They are unbelievably brave under fire, often more so than the Constabulary. Rural Tausug for the most part have accepted Philippine government law largely on their own terms, and for a variety of reasons, both military and political, the government is in no position to force them to accept it.

Unfortunately, the Philippine government's approach to the problem has ignored consideration of the obvious fact that two legal systems are in competition with each other. Rather, efforts have been made to find military solutions, all of which have failed, or stress has been placed upon economic development and "progress" as a means of luring Tausug away from violence. While there are many reasons for the extreme violence in Jolo—most of which we have discussed in this book—, poverty is not one of them. Poverty is, after all, relative to your point of view, and rural poverty is never as bad as urban poverty. I am not sure in what sense rural Tausug can be said to be aware that they are "poor," but it certainly is not the same awareness of poverty felt by a tenant farmer in Luzon. Furthermore, economic development is largely limited to developing exploitation of the sea (tuna and shrimp fishing in particular), and I have considerable doubts about the effect of this upon the interior farmers who comprise the bulk of the population on Jolo. At present, subsistence fishing in Sulu provides a very high protein intake for the average Tausug. Whether large scale commercial fishing developments would spell ecological disaster for the subsistence fishing is a moot point which I cannot answer. My sympathies for the Tausug incline me to seriously question the value of commercial fishing in the long run.

The Trojan horse in this discussion, of course, is the fact that the Western medicine has drastically reduced the infant mortality rate in Sulu, with a consequent rise in population (partially offset by a high death rate from feuding). Economic development of some kind is probably going to be necessary to increase the food supply in the near future—certainly some changes in agricultural technique, like learning to use animal fertilizers on rice fields. Whether economic development is not itself another Trojan horse of a different color is a problem which the Tausug are not alone in facing, and the answers— if indeed there are any—are not easily forthcoming.

Most of the ethnic minorities in the Philippines have been grossly exploited in multifarious ways, but compared to many of the other minorities, the Tausug have not been subjected to this mistreatment. Relations between the Moslems, Chinese, and Christians in the town of Jolo are probably better than any place else in the country, partially because of an absence of serious economic competition. There are no big-time loggers stripping the forests of Jolo as they have done in other minority areas. There are no Christian immigrants to dispossess local owners of ancestral land. There are no huge coconut or abaca plantations exploiting cheap labor. There is no poverty caused by dispossession and exploitation. There is no disillusionment caused by cultural deprivation.

The Tausug have fared this well largely because of their favorable location with an island totally their own, because of their size, and because of their possession of firearms and willingness to use them. In contrast to the relatively peaceful Moslem-Christian relations on Jolo, the situation in many parts of Mindanao has recently escalated (1971) into a vicious war between Moslems and Christian immigrants which has become a major political issue in the Philippines.

There are two major ways in which modern nations have handled the problem of ethnic minorities within their borders. On the one hand, an effort may be made to eliminate minority cultures through education and persuasion, or brute force if all else fails. A small amount of regional diversity may be tolerated to encourage the tourist trade, primarily on the level of quaint marriage customs, native dances, costumes, and the like. The other method is to work toward the achievement of something approaching a federal system in which the substantive reality of cultural difference is encouraged and preserved. For the most part, the Philippines made an implied decision prior to World War II—no doubt based upon the American example—to adopt the first alternative. The Philippines simply does not take ethnic regionalism among its Moslem minorities seriously, and the implied goal (although certainly not a deliberate decision) is to wipe Tausug culture off the map, including its major social and legal institutions, values, and forms of life. It will be allowed to keep its religion, of course, but only in relation to individual rights to worship, not the group rights of the community of the faithful. Moslem theology and political theory are very sensitive to this last distinction.

What the future role of the Tausug—and more generally the Moslem minority of the Philippines—will be in the overall national scene is a question which I would hesitate to answer. I do know what the situation is now, and I am not optimistic that it will change in the near future. Perhaps the best that can be expected is the development of a kind of working misunderstanding between Tausug law and government law, hopefully supplemented by an increase in the quality and sensitivity of the Filipino officials who are forced to deal with the Tausug.

# Glossary

*adat*: Custom, customary behavior.

*agama*: Revealed religion, Islam.

AFFINAL: Pertaining to kinship through marriage (in-laws).

BILATERAL: Kinship reckoning from both the father's and the mother's side.

BRIDEWEALTH: Transfer of property from groom's side to bride's side; opposite of dowry.

CULTURE: Learned behavior patterns shared by a social group. As contrasted with social structure: symbols and values in terms of which experience is interpreted.

CORPORATE GROUP: A group which outlasts the lives of its members, has institutionalized leadership, can own property, and has rights and obligations in a legal sense.

COLLATERAL: Kinship based on lines which have "branched off" at some ancestor, as contrasted with lineal kinsmen who are direct ancestors or descendants.

CONSANGUINE: Kinship by "blood."

*datu*: Aristocrat, member of the highest estate.

EGO: The person from whose vantage point kinship relationships are reckoned.

*karayawan*: Goodness, pleasure, peace.

KINDRED: A bilateral kinship group traced outward from ego.

KINSHIP TERMINOLOGY: The primary names for denoting kinsmen. Usually listed in four sets: reference terms (talking about someone), address terms (talking to someone), consanguine terms, affinal terms.

*maisug*: Brave, fearless, violent.

PATRILINEAL, PATRILATERAL: Tracing kinship, either lineally or laterally, only through male links.

*sara*: Law; more specifically, the Canon Law of Islam.

*sipug*: Shame, embarrassment, loss of self-esteem in front of others.

SOCIAL STRUCTURE: The arrangement of persons into groups and the actual realities of social relationships.

STATE: A corporate political organization having a centralized head, embracing a large number of local communities, and usually asserting total dominance within a territory.

# Recommended Reading

GEERTZ, CLIFFORD, 1960, *The Religion of Java.* Glencoe Ill.: The Free Press.
Although the Javanese are different in many ways from the Tausug, this is one of the few good studies in English of Islam in Southeast Asia.

————, 1968, *Islam Observed.* New Haven: Yale University Press.
A brief, but lucid comparison of Islam in Indonesia and Morocco.

GELLNER, ERNST, 1969, *Saints of the Atlas.* London: Weidenfeld and Nicholson.
An Islamic society in North Africa where religious power provides a unifying framework against a background of rampant feuding.

GULICK, JOHN, 1958, *Indigenous Political Systems of Western Malaya.* London: The Athlone Press.
The traditional Malay sultanates operated rather differently from the Tausug sultante, although much of the symbolism was similar. This is a good study by a social anthropologist.

HEINE-GELDERN, ROBERT, 1956, *Conceptions of State and Kinship in Southeast Asia.* Cornell University: Southeast and Asia Data Paper # 18.
A classic analysis of the symbolism of the state in Southeast Asia, involving the correspondence between the microcosm and the macrocosm.

KIEFER, THOMAS M., 1970, Modes of Social Action in Armed Combat. *Journal of the Royal Anthropological Institute,* Volume V, No. 4.
A more extensive analysis of rationality in Tausug warfare.

————, 1970, *The Tausug of Sulu: Moslems of the Southern Philippines* (33⅓ rpm record). New York: Anthology Records.
Tausug instrumental and vocal music, with extensive notes, including a complete epic song.

LANDE, CARL, 1965, *Leaders, Factions and Parties—The Structure of Philippine Politics.* Yale University Southeast Asia Studies 6.
An interesting analysis of Philippine electoral politics, developing the theory of dyadic ties which was used in this book.

RAHMAN, FAZLUR, 1966, *Islam.* New York: Holt, Rinehart, and Winston, Inc. (also released by Anchor Books in paperback, 1968).
An objective and comprehensive introduction to the Moslem religion, primarily in the Near East.

SALEEBY, NAJEEB M., 1908, *The History of Sulu.* Manila: Philippine Bureau of Science, Division of Ethnography Publications, vol. 4, part 2.
Older ethnohistory of the region, quite dated, but still useful.

TARLING, NICHOLAS, 1963, *Piracy and Politics in the Malay World.* Melbourne: F. W. Cheshire.
Although Euro-centered, this is about the only comprehensive history of the fascinating subject of piracy in insular Southeast Asia.